METADRAMA
IN
SHAKESPEARE'S
HENRIAD

METADRAMA
IN
SHAKESPEARE'S
HENRIAD

Richard II
to *Henry* V

JAMES L. CALDERWOOD

University of California Press
Berkeley
Los Angeles
London

University of California Press
Berkeley and Los Angeles, California

University of California Press, Ltd.
London, England

Copyright © 1979 by
The Regents of
the University of California

ISBN 0–520–03652–2
Library of Congress
Catalog Card Number: 77–93467
Printed in
the United States of America

1 2 3 4 5 6 7 8 9

for Cleo

BY MINE HONOUR, IN TRUE ENGLISH

Contents

PREFACE   ix

INTRODUCTION   1

1

Richard II to *Henry IV:*
Variations on the Fall   10

2

Henry IV: The Ascendance of the Lie   30

3

Henry IV: Counterfeit Kings
and Creative Succession   47

4

1 *Henry IV:* Art's Gilded Lie   68

5

2 *Henry IV:* The Embodied Name
and the Rejected Mask   88

6

1 and 2 *Henry IV:* Successive Form
and the Redeemed Word   105

7

Henry V: The Act of Order   134

8

Henry V: English, Rhetoric, Theater   162

APPENDIX: Elizabethan Naming   183

INDEX   221

Preface

I am obliged to Arthur F. Kinney of the *English Literary Renaissance* for permission to reprint in revised form "1 *Henry IV*: Art's Gilded Lie," *English Literary Renaissance* 3, 1 (Winter 1973). I am grateful to Murray Krieger, good friend and colleague, who was typically generous with his time and knowledge; to Jackson I. Cope, good friend and ruthless critic, who supplied a helpful reading of the text; and to Professor Ulrich Knoepflmacher, informal editor for the University of California Press, who made valuable suggestions for a final revision of the early chapters. Whatever transient truths and deathless errors remain in the book are on their heads as well.

The texts referred to throughout are those in *The Complete Plays and Poems of William Shakespeare*, ed. William A. Neilson and Charles J. Hill (Cambridge, Mass., 1942).

Introduction

This book examines Shakespeare's second historical tetralogy—*The Henriad*, as Alvin B. Kernan has happily phrased it[1]—as a relatively self-contained metadrama in which the playwright subjects the nature and materials of his art to radical scrutiny. This is a fairly late-arriving approach to the plays. E. M. W. Tillyard regarded the transition from *Richard II* to *Henry V* as an epic representation of England's passage from medieval to Renaissance culture, from feudal monarchy to Machiavellian realpolitik.[2] Lily B. Campbell, on the other hand, saw the plays as reflecting not cultural developments of England's past, but specific political problems of Elizabeth's day; for her they were "mirrors of Elizabethan policy."[3] J. Dover Wilson believed that the two central plays constituted "Shakespeare's great morality play," with Prince Hal playing Everyman to Falstaff's Vanity, Hotspur's Chivalry,

1. Alvin B. Kernan, "*The Henriad*: Shakespeare's Major History Plays," in *Modern Shakespearean Criticism*, ed. Alvin B. Kernan (New York, 1970), pp. 245–275.
2. E. M. W. Tillyard, *Shakespeare's History Plays* (London, 1944).
3. Lily B. Campbell, *Shakespeare's Histories: Mirrors of Elizabethan Policy* (San Marino, Calif., 1947).

1

and the Lord Chief Justice's Rule of the Law.[4] In contrast to Wilson's allegorical reading, Derek Traversi advocated a "more directly 'dramatic' approach," by which he meant a realistic concern for the blood-and-leather texture of history.[5] From these, and a great many other studies, have emerged sensible and insightful discussions of the moral and political themes of the plays, of their imagery, structural interrelations, and characters.[6] At the same time, such critics have for

4. J. Dover Wilson, *The Fortunes of Falstaff* (Cambridge, 1943).

5. Derek Traversi, *Shakespeare: From Richard II to Henry V* (Stanford, 1957), Preface.

6. Prominent among those who have written on *The Henriad* are Tillyard (see note 2); John Palmer, *Political Characters of Shakespeare* (London, 1945); Campbell (see note 3); Irving Ribner, *The English History Play in the Age of Shakespeare* (Princeton, 1957); Traversi (see note 5); Z. Stribrny, *Shakespeare's History Plays* (Prague, 1959); M. M. Reese, *The Cease of Majesty* (London, 1961); L. C. Knights, *William Shakespeare, The Histories* (London, 1962); H. M. Richmond, *Shakespeare's Political Plays* (New York, 1967); J. Winny, *The Player King* (London, 1968); Robert Ornstein, *A Kingdom for a Stage* (Cambridge, Mass., 1972); John C. Bromley, *The Shakespearean Kings* (Boulder, Colo., 1971); Robert B. Pierce, *Shakespeare's History Plays: The Family and the State* (Columbus, Ohio, 1971); Michael Manheim, *The Weak King Dilemma in the Shakespearean History Play* (Syracuse, 1973); and Moody E. Prior, *The Drama of Power: Studies in Shakespeare's History Plays* (Evanston, Ill., 1973).

Some shorter pieces that I have found especially impressive and useful—and I can by no means claim to have read all of the criticism on the plays—are A. P. Rossiter's "Ambivalence: The Dialectic of the Histories," in his *Angel with Horns* (London, 1951); C. L. Barber's "Rule and Misrule in *Henry IV*," in his *Shakespeare's Festive Comedy*

the most part let Shakespeare's dramatic medium go largely unremarked.

The most prominent—certainly, as the plays have come down to us, the most available—feature of that dramatic medium is its language. The First Folios abide our scrutiny, the First Performances have jigged their way with Kempe and Heminges and Phillips out of the world and time. As a result, some recent critics have given special attention to language in *The Henriad*— not language as a means of representation, a window onto subject matter, but language as an object of representation. Joan Webber, for instance, observes that *The Henriad* "is, among other things, an analysis of the nature of kingship and royal rhetoric which directly concerns the relationship between language and reality."[7] Eric La Guardia focuses less directly on lan-

---

(Princeton, 1959); Joan Webber's "The Renewal of the King's Symbolic Role: From *Richard II* to *Henry V*," *Texas Studies in Literature and Language* 4 (1963); Harold E. Toliver's "Falstaff, the Prince, and the History Play," *Shakespeare Quarterly* 16 (Winter 1965); Eric La Guardia's "Ceremony and History: The Problem of Symbol from *Richard II* to *Henry V*," in *Pacific Coast Studies in Shakespeare*, ed. Waldo F. McNeir and Thelma N. Greenfield (Eugene, Ore., 1966); Leonard Dean's "From *Richard II* to *Henry V*: A Closer View," in *Studies in Honor of DeWitt T. Starnes*, ed. Thomas P. Harrison and James H. Sledd (Austin, Texas, 1967); Sigurd Burckhardt's " 'Swoll'n with Some Other Grief': Shakespeare's Prince Hal Trilogy," in his *Shakespearean Meanings* (Princeton, 1968); Alvin B. Kernan's article (see note 1); and John W. Blanpied's " 'Unfathered heirs and loathly births of nature': Bringing History to Crisis in 2 *Henry IV*," *English Literary Renaissance* 5, 2 (Spring 1975).

7. Joan Webber (see note 6 above), p. 530.

guage than on the evolution of cultural symbolism, finding that "what organizes the elements of the entire drama is the movement from medieval figural reality (in which a rigid analogical connection between God and nature is maintained) toward a more secular view of reality (in which the divine analogy is superseded by the importance of immediate, contingent circumstances of nature)."[8] Or, as Alvin Kernan says, "In the most summary terms [*The Henriad* presents us with] a movement from ceremony and ritual to history."[9]

The work of these and other critics—Leonard Dean and Sigurd Burckhardt, for instance[10]—provides, I think, a definitive study of the shifts and turns of symbolism in the four plays. My own approach is less consistently devoted to language than theirs—chapter 4, for instance, is wholly concerned with dramatic illusion, and much of the final three chapters deals with the nature of dramatic form, with the role of the dramatist, and with theatrical mimesis—and rather more consistently devoted to the self-reflexive aspects of the plays. For example, whereas Webber finds Shakespeare employing royal symbolism in "an effort to solve a political problem through creative use of language,"[11] my tendency is to reverse the priorities. Instead of regarding language as a means toward political ends, I would find Shakespeare solving problems of language by means of politics. Political affairs, in other words, become metaphors for art.

8. Eric La Guardia (see note 6 above), p. 69.
9. Alvin Kernan (see note 1 above), p. 246.
10. See note 6 above.
11. Joan Webber, p. 530.

This kind of metaphoric projection seems natural enough; most men's professional concerns get smuggled into other areas of their lives by metaphoric conveyances. Surgeons must think more than other men of incisive actions and of ruptured relationships in need of suturing, architects of friendships solidly founded and buttressed, painters of the composition of a morning and the hues of emotion. It is hardly surprising that a playwright like Shakespeare would project his concerns about drama not only into life but even into the fictional life of his plays, where the world may become a stage, history a plot, kings dramatists, courtiers actors, commoners audiences, and speech itself the dialogue or script that gives breath to all the rest.

In *The Henriad* the main metadramatic plot centers in the "fall of speech." To the Divine Rightness of Richard's kingship corresponds a kind of language in which words have an inalienable right to their meanings, even a divine right insofar as God is the ultimate guarantor of verbal truth. In this sacramental language of Richard's imagination God is an invisible third partner to every dialogue, the final verbal authority, even as He is the invisible third partner in every trial by combat, the final judgmental authority. Richard's sentimental, magical investment in royal semantics metaphorically reflects Shakespeare's own artistic investment in the poetic mode and in a language of ontological rightness, a language of "names." Not that Richard in any blunt sense "is" Shakespeare—though he is surely his imaginative possession—for it is Shakespeare, after all, who supplies us with a critique of Richard's position. Metaphors are metaphors, in short, not allegorical equations.

For God as the third partner in dialogue Boling-broke substitutes material force, human need, "votes." The determinant of meaning is now, like the occupant of a throne, whoever gets there first with the most. When Richard and Bolingbroke meet at Flint Castle, the royal name so tenuously held by Richard is without meaning, and the forceful meaning of Bolingbroke is without the royal name. Words and meanings generally are now disjunct. In the "base court" (appropriately) the third partner to Richard's and Bolingbroke's dialogue, the verbal authority, is not God but Bolingbroke's twenty thousand silent soldiers, who help seize the word "king" and give it the new meaning of "Henry IV." This "debasement" of kingship involves the secularizing of language as well, the surrender of a sacramental language to a utilitarian one in which the relation between words and things is arbitrary, unsure, and ephemeral.

Bolingbroke's usurpation of the name "king" brings into dramatic being both the lie and metaphor. Falstaff, the corporealized lie, is also a low-life metaphor for kingship, as at a higher level is Hotspur, "king of honor." Prince Hal begins his ascent toward the throne as an apparent lie, the wastrel truant. And in the person of Henry IV the lie is on the throne of England. Even the dramatist Shakespeare must seem a liar, now that truth, meaning, and value are no longer naturally resident in words. Thus he and Hal, the interior dramatist, begin their plays as seeming liars and seek to transcend the fallen, lie-fraught world of Henry IV by restoring value and meaning both to kingship and to the King's English.

In the *Henry IV* plays the redemption of the word

is commercially figured as the paying of verbal debts, by Hal, "who never promiseth but he means to pay" (5.4.43), and by Shakespeare, whose successful dramatic form depends on his fulfillment of structural promises. A lie is the price of bribing the temporarily rebellious Falstaff to reenter the illusion of history in 1 *Henry IV*: "For my part, if a lie may do thee grace, / I'll gild it with the happiest terms I have" (5.4.161–162). And a more heinous lie is the price of subduing the rebel forces at the "battle" of Gaultree Forest in 2 *Henry IV*. In this break-faith world one word is made good—Hal's promise to redeem time when men think least he will, particularly the implicit promise of his quiet reply to Falstaff's "Banish plump Jack, and banish all the world"—"I do, I will" (2.4.526–528). A fuller redemption of speech is accomplished in *Henry V*. There the divinely guaranteed truths of Richard's reign and the ubiquitous lies of Henry's are succeeded by rhetoric, the language of conquest. The rhetorical word is no longer instinct with value, as in Richard's time, nor divorced from it, as in Henry's, but triumphant over it. In rhetoric, words take on an achieved, pragmatic value as instruments of persuasive action, even as English kingship takes on an earned, human value by virtue of Harry's victory at Agincourt. But Shakespeare's verbal achievement is no more enduring than Harry's brief reign; it is a fugitive solution to linguistic and dramatic enigmas that will vex the playwright to the end of his career.

If the fall and partial recovery of speech constitutes the metadramatic mainplot, there are a few subplots as well. For instance, the self-reflexiveness of drama creates a minor comic crisis in 1 *Henry IV* when Falstaff threatens at Shrewsbury to secede from fiction and expose drama as a fraud. To restore unity to the play Hal must sacrifice not only the newly won honor of killing Hotspur but, by lying, his own honesty as well. In *Henry V* Shakespeare's pursuit of dramatic unity, which mirrors Harry's pursuit of national unity in England, puts the dramatist's honor in jeopardy. In this plight, Shakespeare must side with Falstaff, elevating the old warrior's cry of theatrical fraud at Shrewsbury into an official postulate of the play itself, as proclaimed by the Chorus. With this admission that theater is a lie—and by a similar metaphoric admission within the play—Shakespeare avoids dishonesty by publicizing its presence. From a too easy concept of dramatic order, characterized by authorial chauvinism, he wrests a new kind of order in which the playwright adopts the paradoxical role of impartial partisan.

One aspect of the fall of speech in *The Henriad*—its relation to linguistic developments during Shakespeare's time—has only been touched on in the text itself. I believe, however, that in the transition from Richard's magical to Bolingbroke's pragmatic language Shakespeare has dramatized—has in Eliseo Vivas's terms, made "insistent"—a shift in the nature of symbolism that was "subsistent," that had not fully surfaced, in the culture of his day. That shift was an intensified version of what, over the long course of verbal history, Ernst Cassirer has divided into three phases—mimetic, analogical, and symbolic.[12] In the mimetic phase, primitive speech reflects—by onomatopoesis and similar means—the sensory impression of objects

12. Ernst Cassirer, *The Philosophy of Symbolic Forms* (New Haven, Conn., 1953), Vol. 1, *Language*, pp. 186–198.

so that the word as nearly as possible *is* the thing. In the analogical phase, words become detached from their referents, no longer directly resembling them, but associated by parallelism and correlation. Finally, in the symbolic phase, words are signs wholly unrelated to the meanings arbitrarily assigned to them. In the Appendix, "Elizabethan Naming," I have tried, with a great show of learning, to make a rough chart of this development as it was occurring in the sixteenth and seventeenth centuries. But such a chart, however relevant as historical background, is better relegated to the back of a book whose primary interest is not in seeing how these four plays illustrate the culture of Shakespeare's age but in showing how they comprise a coherent exploration of the nature and materials of the playwright's art.

Richard II TO *Henry IV:*

VARIATIONS ON THE FALL

As the deposed Richard II sits alone at Pomfret Castle musing on his losses, his only apparent consolation is an abundance of metaphors bestowed upon him by a generous playwright. The most extravagant of these is his sustained conceit identifying himself as Time's "numbering clock":

> I wasted time, and now doth Time waste me,
> For now hath Time made me his numbering clock.
> My thoughts are minutes, and with sighs they jar
> Their watches on unto mine eyes, the outward watch,
> Whereto my finger, like a dial's point,
> Is pointing still, in cleansing them from tears.
> Now sir, the sound that tells what hour it is
> Are clamorous groans, which strike upon my heart,
> Which is the bell. So sighs and tears and groans
> Show minutes, times, and hours. But my time
> Runs posting on in Bolingbroke's proud joy
> While I stand fooling here, his Jack o' the clock.
>
> (5.5.49–60)

The ironies of the time-waster now wasted by time, though they eloquently express the pathos of Richard's plight, seem a small semantic return on a poetic investment of twelve lines. However, if the plight of the unemployed sovereign in prison figures that of *his* sovereign, the poet-playwright Shakespeare, then at that level of interpretation this clock may tell us more than timely truths.

In the first place, as "teller" (line 55), that is, as true reflector or measuring device, the clock as such is notoriously prone to error, especially in an England that had yet to establish Greenwich as a final temporal authority (even though another great temporal authority, Elizabeth, was born there). In the second place, though Shakespeare probably considered time as part of the natural cosmic order, he could hardly help knowing that of all temporal units the "minutes, times, and hours" he emphasizes here are the most arbitrary— since days, months, seasons, and years are at least based on periodicity in nature. This stress upon the arbitrary and distorting features of temporal representation is reinforced by the fact that Richard's bodily clock reflects his internal state, so that the external representation of time (the "outward watch" of eyes, finger, heart) is governed by the subjective experience of time. The overall effect of the conceit is to bring home to us the extent to which time is humanly created rather than mimetically measured, and hence how fundamentally cut off from time man is. The temporal *Ding an sich* is presumably out there somewhere, but it is available to man only through the deflecting prism of his symbolic representations. The clock thus asserts the disjunction of man and nature (time) at the very moment that it serves imperfectly to unite the two.

The wayward artificiality of the clock as a teller of nature's truths is mirrored verbally by the strained, rhetorical self-consciousness (for example, "Now sir") of Richard's conceit telling of the clock. All of Rich-

ard's metaphors during the latter part of the play and
especially at Pomfret Castle exhibit this air of uneasy
contrivance. As metaphors they appear to assert an
equation of tenor and vehicle—usually of Richard and
the world outside his prison—much as the clock presents itself as a true teller of time. But they are metaphors in which Richard no longer believes, and which
therefore imply a chasm between him and the world in
the very attempt to bridge it:

> I have been studying how I may compare
> This prison where I live unto the world.
> And for because the world is populous
> And here is not a creature but myself,
> I cannot do it. Yet *I'll hammer it out*.
> My brain I'll prove the female to my soul,
> My soul the father, and these two beget
> A generation of *still-breeding thoughts*,
> And these same thoughts people this little world
> In humours *like* the people of this world.
>
> (5.5.1–10; my italics)

What Richard hammers out as a labor of will rather
than of belief is a series of metaphoric likenesses whose
ambiguous success in connecting him to the world outside is indicated by the fact that they will prove "still-
breeding"—ever-and-never-breeding at once, always-
bearing and yet stillborn.[1] Ultimately, however, Richard's thoughts can populate only "this little world," the
nursery of his own mind, unable to pass beyond like-

---

1. Eric La Guardia, "Ceremony and History: The Prob-
lem of Symbol from *Richard II* to *Henry V*," in *Pacific Coast
Studies in Shakespeare*, ed. Waldo F. McNeir and Thelma
N. Greenfield (Eugene, Ore., 1966), p. 74.

ness and become authentic citizens in the larger world outside. Metaphors, after all, are not the thing itself.

Symbols had not always seemed so isolated from reality. Indeed, on Richard's unexamined assumptions, language had been bonded to nature and the world order by virtue of God's certification of him as a Divine Right king. The original power of the divine Word remained actively at work in the King's English, just as divine authority descending by way of primogeniture was immanent in Richard himself. But it is the purpose of the play to divest Richard of these views—to drive a wedge between words and their meanings, between the world order and the word order, between the king and the man who is king, and between names and metaphors. Thus we find in *Richard II* not merely the fall of a king but also the fall of kingly speech—of a speech conceived of as sacramental and ontological, in which words are not proxies for things but part of the things themselves. With the fall of this King's English there falls also a view of reality contained within it, a view so similar to the "world picture" attributed to Elizabeth's reign that the parallels might well seem vexing to anyone who worked in words. "I am Richard II," Elizabeth told William Lombarde, "Know ye not that?" In 1595 Elizabeth had not yet played Richard II to Essex's Bolingbroke, but her language—the English on which playwrights like Shakespeare drew—was already beginning to play Richard II to Sir Francis Bacon's Bolingbroke. In the Appendix, "Elizabethan Naming," I have outlined this general shift from verbal fideism to skepticism during the sixteenth and seventeenth centuries. Shakespeare, however, comes at these matters dramatically. Like Richard in Pomfret Castle, he addresses himself not to linguistic theory, but to homelier things like names and metaphors.

*

Losing his name, Richard loses everything. Cast out of his medieval world of preestablished order and significance, he is isolated in Pomfret Castle where he attempts, with stiff rhetorical flourishes, to hammer out meanings that had once simply been there for his taking. His resort to metaphor is inevitable once the old names are gone, for metaphor is the language of the unnamed. The process is familiar. Lacking a vocabulary for the unnamed, we steal from the already named. Each successful new metaphor is a creative insight and for a time gives off a spark of aesthetic pleasure. So long as tension exists between tenor and vehicle—so long as there is an element of the negative in our awareness that it is not what it literally claims to be—the metaphor remains metaphoric. With wear, however, this tension slackens, and the metaphor collapses into an inert name—or more familiarly "dies." Thus few people today hear the "call" of the word *vocation* or feel the "fusion of self and god" in *enthusiasm*. The fact that *baron* once meant roughly "blockhead" had been forgotten even by Shakespeare's time, when noble reminders still abounded. Language, in short, is a cemetery of dead metaphors, as linguists are fond of saying; or as poets like Emerson prefer, it is fossil poetry.

In a sense metaphor is an improper use of words, a violation of the linguistic system. Its depth structure is that of the proposition "A is B"—"Honey is sweet"

—whether the tenor is present or only implied in the surface structure. But whereas none of the properties of sweetness is incompatible with honey, a metaphor cannot be a metaphor unless some, perhaps most, of its properties are incompatible with its subject. "For what els is your Metaphor," Puttenham asks, "but an inversion of sense by transport."[2] For this reason a metaphor may initially look like a terminological error, a misnaming. When Mistress Quickly cries out to the street-fighting Falstaff "Ah thou honey-suckle vil-lain!" and again "Thou art a honey-seed," we may spend some long moments puzzling over the honeylike properties of plump Jack before realizing that Mistress Quickly is playing hostess not to metaphor but to malapropism. She means, not "honey-suckle" and "honey-seed," but "homicidal" and "homicide" (2 *Hen. IV*, 2.1.55, 59).

In Mistress Quickly's usage, error must be distin-guished from apparent metaphor. Normally, it is the other way round: metaphor must earn its title to truth

2. *Elizabethan Critical Essays*, ed. G. Gregory Smith (London, 1904), 2:160. Puttenham's view that figures are trespasses of speech, and my own emphasis in this chapter on metaphor as a violation of the linguistic system, should be qualified to take account of the fact that language so abounds with figurative speech that we can hardly call it a deviation from the norm. Metaphor is a trespass insofar as it is nonlogical; it says what literally is not. But a very great deal of language is nonlogical in this sense. Moreover, some metaphors, truly creative, name the previously un-named—get a line on aspects of experience and reality that lie quite outside the received vocabulary of a culture. Others, however, simply rename the already named; they are not exploratory but inventive, products of Coleridge's Fancy rather than Imagination.

in a contest against error. Any new metaphor must be tested, must win its way to acceptance, its truth competing for favor against the odds of its own more obvious falseness. When in 1 *Henry IV* Falstaff calls Mistress Quickly an otter, Hal challenges the term— "An otter, Sir John! Why an otter?"—thus forcing Falstaff to defend the truth of his metaphor: "Why, she's neither fish nor flesh; a man knows not where to have her" (3.3.142–145). Mistress Quickly bustles forth a convincing denial—"Thou or any man knows where to have me, thou knave, thou!" (3.3.147)—but the point is that the question of truth has arisen.

The question of truth is precisely what does not arise in the case of dead metaphors. Here, the vehicle is no longer an illuminating similitude but literally the name of the tenor. No one questions whether "far-seeing" is an appropriate term for the broadcasting of images by radiowaves to receivers that project them onto a picture tube. When the semantic batteries in a metaphor have gone entirely dead, as those of "television" have for most people and certainly for those to whom it is merely "TV," the metaphor ceases to be a metaphor and becomes a name. As such, it passes securely beyond challenges as to its truth, rightness, and acceptability. Had Falstaff said "Francis Bacon is a baron," Hal would no more have thought to challenge the dead metaphor—"A baron, Sir John! Why a baron?"—than he would to challenge the proper name, "Why 'Francis Bacon'?" To either question the only possible answer, even for a master of improvisation like Falstaff, would be a shrugging "That's simply the name." There is no relevance to search out, no insightful comparison or "before unapprehended relation of things." A name is a name is a name.

Now for Richard II kingship, *his* kingship, is as much beyond question as a proper name. It has the automatic warrant of Divine Right, which means not that Richard conceives of himself as the right king but that he conceives of himself simply as *the* king. For him "King" and "Richard" are not two words but one indissoluble name. The old metaphors linking kingly office and divine office are not analogical truths in Richard's imagination but anagogic ones, not metaphors but identities. The king is not *like*, he *is* the "deputy elected by the Lord," "God's substitute," "the Lord's lieutenant," and so on. And because "King" and "Richard" are one entity, Richard is all of these things—and so he must carry his title with him to the grave, all successors disallowed.

This seems to be why Shakespeare, despite having established (in act 1, scene 2 especially) Richard's criminal failures, even his murderousness, as king, then dramatizes his deposition not so much as a trial of Richard's conduct as a trial of his concept of the royal office. At issue is whether King and Richard are in fact one word and whether the metaphors so royally taken for granted are literally true. Thus Shakespeare charts Richard's dramatic experience by the coordinates of name and person, thrusting him from a belief in the monistic divinity of name—

> Arm, arm, my name! A puny subject strikes
> At thy great glory
>
> (3.2.86–87)

—to a recognition of dualistic separability—

> What must the King do now? Must he submit?
> The king shall do it. Must he be deposed?
> The King shall be contented. Must he lose
> The name of king? O' God's name, let it go!
> (3.3.143–146)

—to an ultimate loss of name and a consequent disso-
lution of personal identity and meaning—

> I have no name, no title;
> No, not that name was given me at the font,
> But 'tis usurped. Alack the heavy day,
> That I have worn so many winters out
> And know not what name to call myself!
> (4.1.255–259)

Ernst Cassirer remarks that, among primitives,
"the being and life of a person are so intimately connected with his name that, as long as the name is preserved and spoken, its bearer is still felt to be present
and directly active."[3] In Richard's case the ambiguity
of the life-giving powers of the name is given full expression. Richard "lives" only so long as his name is
honored; once that is gone, he becomes in his own
word "nothing," even before his death at the hands of
Exton. In Pomfret Castle he realizes that the name of
king is merely arbitrary, that he has an identity apart
from the name. Yet this knowledge, instead of sustaining him, instead of making him feel that he has lost
"merely" a name and not life itself, destroys him.
There are no "mere" words, it seems, only meaningful

3. Ernst Cassirer, *Language and Myth* (New York, 1946),
p. 52.

ones. Exton kills a man who is, in his namelessness, already dead.

*

Richard's world is dead too. It is a world conceived of in metaphors that had died into names, as Richard discovered too late. The metaphors he has taken literally were also taken literally in the sixteenth century, and implicit in them was a world view. Pattrick Cruttwell remarks:

> Shakespeare is not really a philosopher; he had no philosophy of his own. He didn't need to have one; it was given him. He had simply to describe human life as honestly, vividly, and completely as he knew, and then, through the very terms of reference by which alone he *could* describe it, a philosophy emerges.[4]

The philosophy that emerges, Cruttwell says, is the "integrated medieval view" that E. M. W. Tillyard has more famously, if somewhat metachronically, called the Elizabethan world picture. This world view, inherited from medieval culture, was intimately bound up with Elizabethan language, also inherited from medieval culture. The conception of a world essentially animistic, full of anthropomorphic life, dancing, ceremony, order, harmony—a hierarchical world of Platonic dualities and microspheres fashioned on the principles of analogy and parallelism—this world was not merely a set of theories in which men believed; it

4. Pattrick Cruttwell, "Physiology and Psychology in Shakespeare's Age," *Journal of the History of Ideas* 12 (Jan. 1951): 75–89.

was what most of their key words implicitly *meant*. The world picture was a word picture. It was not for nothing that reality was thought to be composed of "elements" and nature conceived of as a "book."

But in Richard's dramatic experience—as in England's historical experience during the sixteenth and seventeenth centuries—the Book of Nature becomes incomprehensible. Things no longer answer to their assigned names. Once upon a time, in a fairytale world, "four lagging winters and four wanton springs [could be made to] end in a word, such [was] the breath of kings" (1.3.214–215). Once upon a time the king's name was twenty thousand names, and the king and God were consubstantial. That fairytale time had its historical counterpart in Shakespeare's England, as the fictive Richard had his real-life spokesman in, among others, William Tyndale, who said that

> he that judgeth the King judgeth God, and he that layeth hands on the King layeth hands on God, and he that resisteth the King resisteth God. . . . The King is in this world without law, and he may at his lust do right or wrong and shall give accounts but to God only.[5]

These claims echo again and again through the Tudor homilies, especially in that "Concernyng Good Ordre and Obedience to Rulers and Magistrates" (1547) and that "Against Disobedience and Wilful Rebellion" (1574).[6] That kingship confers quasi-divine status and

5. Quoted by Philip Wheelwright in *The Burning Fountain* (Bloomington, Ind., 1954), p. 215.

6. To be sure, the increased stress in the sixteenth century on the divinity of kingship need not entail an increased belief in the concept, much less an exceptionally godlike

inviolability upon its holder is owing in part to God's direct appointment of kings, an appointment renewed through primogeniture, and in part to God's establishment of hierarchical order throughout the universe. As the visible symbol of human order, the king mediates between "earthly men" and both God and God's grand design. If he falls, all else falls with him, as Ulysses, the domino theorist of *Troilus and Cressida*, so eloquently details it.

Bishop Carlisle, the Ulysses of *Richard II*, sounds a similar theme. Just before the deposition of Richard, when Bolingbroke says "In God's name, I'll ascend the regal throne," Carlisle cries "Marry, God forbid!" and in effect reads the Tudor homilies to him:

> . . . shall the figure of God's majesty,
> His captain, steward, deputy elect,
> Anointed, crowned, planted many years,
> Be judged by subject and inferior breath,
> And he himself not present?
>
> (4.1.125–129)

The Earl of Northumberland applauds Carlisle's performance—"Well have you argued, sir"—but adds,

---

crop of kings. The homily "Against Disobedience and Wilful Rebellion" (1574) was issued not as a spontaneous expression of belief in the divinity of Elizabeth but as a propagandistic response to the Northern Uprising of 1569. With the horrors of the civil wars still alive in public memory, both commoner and king wanted sacred as well as secular support for the established order. Even so, need is the fuel of belief, none more powerful, and it is quite impossible to dismiss the enormous prestige that monarchy had for men like Ascham, Spenser, Hooker, and Bacon, or to ignore the ubiquitous metaphors linking order in the state with divine orderings of the universe and the laws of nature.

"and for your pains / Of capital treason we arrest you here" (4.1.150–151). So much, it would seem, for Divine Right!

And so much, also, for a sacramental language in which words have a kind of divine, inalienable right to their referents. Unlike Richard, Bolingbroke has never subscribed to such a language. From the opening scene of the play he has regarded words as mere vocal conveniences whose substance lies not in themselves but in what they designate. Thus he employs words as promissory notes in gathering followers in his venture for kingship, and reinforces what few words he does utter with material force. At Flint Castle, where Richard descends to the base court with many words and few soldiers, Bolingbroke listens politely and says little: his twenty thousand soldiers are all the eloquence he requires. If Richard is a regal name that is gradually divested of its meaning, Bolingbroke is a kind of material force or meaning in search of the name that will give him public expression.

The name Bolingbroke seeks is, of course, "king," and the bond between word and meaning is analogous to that between kingship and the holder of that office. If the king's name or title normally goes unquestioned, it is not, Richard discovers, because it is divinely guaranteed but because it is humanly conferred and assumed. Names fit their referents not because of an underlying correspondence or substantive unity but by virtue of informal covenants among speakers. Kings and meanings rule by custom. It follows, as Bolingbroke well knows, that the name of "king" will as readily answer to the meaning of "Henry IV" as to that of "Richard II." The next step in this reduction of language from the sacrosanct to the purely arbitrary is registered by Falstaff's remark to Prince Hal at the opening of 1 *Henry IV*: "I would to God thou and I knew where a commodity of good names were to be bought" (1.2.92–94). Like money, language is now reckoned a merely useful social instrument. Its meaning and value are no longer intrinsic but manufactured in response to the vicissitudes of the marketplace. In the inflationary times of 2 *Henry IV* the value of the word will fall still further. But that is to get ahead of the story.

When words are divorced from things, when names are seen to have neither a magical nor an inherently natural connection to their referents, then meaning comes into question, both in language and in kingship. What, during the reign of Bolingbroke, does the name of "king" mean? *Richard II* has presented us with the gradual estrangement of the name "king" from the meaning which, in the person of Richard himself, it has expressed, a meaning underwritten by God. If the royal name still presumes to mean "the Lord's lieutenant" or "God's substitute," then the proposition "The King is Henry IV" can only be a lie, as Hotspur and the other conspirators feel. If, on the other hand, the proposition is true, if Bolingbroke *is* "King Henry IV," then the old meanings are, and must always have been, not literal but only metaphorical. If so, the king is not a participant in divinity but an actor in a secular role, as Richard appears to realize in his tiring-room at Pomfret Castle:

> Thus play I in one person many people,
> And none contented. Sometimes am I king,

Then treasons make me wish myself a beggar,
And so I am. Then crushing penury
Persuades me I was better when a king;
Then am I kinged again—and by and by
Think that I am unkinged by Bolingbroke,
And straight am nothing.

(5.5.31–38)

Richard's world of names has cracked apart to reveal the metaphor that was inert but not entirely dead within. Between "king" and such meanings as "God's substitute" stands, not an equals sign, but an "as-if." If what is true of the king's name is also true of the King's English—or, in Shakespeare's time, of the Queen's English—then the implications for the poet-playwright are inauspicious indeed.

*

Why, we may wonder, should Shakespeare fashion in *Richard II* not merely the fall of a king but also the fall of kingly speech? Kings have died from time to time and worms have eaten them, but not for words. Henry VI, Richard III, and John, all fall without our feeling that a world of words topples with them. Yet there is clearly a sense in which Richard's verbal experience can be seen to reflect issues of paramount interest to the poet-playwright. Indeed, Richard has often been called a poet-king, not because he speaks excellent verse—as the "unpoetic" Bolingbroke does also—but because his attitude toward language is poetic. After his return from Ireland, he ignores his captains' calls to action, preferring instead to "sit upon the ground / And tell sad stories of the deaths of kings" (3.3.155–156). That is, rather than enter on actions that would assert his authority in England, Richard lapses into forms of lyric narcissism. These sentimental verbal kingdoms are gratifying to him because within their imagined borders he holds uncontested sway; no Bolingbroke may enter there.

It is not quite accurate, however, to say that the poetic Richard whiles away his time with symbols and ceremonies at the expense of reality and action, which fall under the aegis of Bolingbroke, because in Richard's view language participates in reality, and words constitute actions. Yet Richard's journey through the play from Windsor Castle to Pomfret Castle, from Highness to nothingness, dramatizes the breakdown of this conception of symbolism and language. He experiences in miniature the whole cultural metamorphosis of language, the long historical process in which the marriage of word and thing, signifier and signified, was put asunder and man's thought divorced from his world. For Bacon, Hobbes, the Royal Society, and modern linguists, this process is a melioristic one—not a breakdown of the union between word and thing but a liberation of the word from the thing.[7] For the poet, however, such a process is analogous to the Fall—or, in *Richard II*, to the deposition of a Divine Right king. For if language even in its post-Edenic, fallen form

7. As I mentioned in the Introduction (pp. 8–9), Ernst Cassirer regards this linguistic development as a three-phase movement from a "mimetic" through an "analogical" to a "symbolic" relationship between signs and meanings. He sees this process as a teleological maturing of language, an achievement of "inner freedom." See his *The Philosophy of Symbolic Forms* (New Haven, Conn., 1953), vol. 1, *Language*, pp. 186–198.

were sacramental—if its words either contained divinity, as in the figure of Christ the Logos, or even represented divinity, as in the figure of the Divine Right monarch—then the man who held dominion over language—whether king, priest, magician, or poet—would in some degree hold dominion over things and men's minds as well. Merely by practicing his craft the poet would participate in the divine order, bringing the Book of Art into direct alignment with the Book of Nature, and acquiring by virtue of his mastery of words something of the creative authority deeply embedded in them from the beginning. He would then rebut the philistine claim that poetry is a pleasant lie, not by saying with Sidney that the poet nothing affirmeth and hence cannot lie, but by saying that his loving attendance upon language affirms a divine order and truth already implicit in words.

But for poet as well as king, it is not so. In *Richard II* Shakespeare dramatizes his awareness that his verbal medium is founded not on names but on metaphor. More precisely, within a language of names, seemingly bonded to Elizabethan reality and warranted by God, lies the altogether human presence of metaphor, its once creative energy long since hardened into conventional definition.[8] This descent from names to meta-

8. In discovering the metaphor within the name, Shakespeare could be said to have recognized something like the so-called Sapir-Whorf hypothesis, according to which each distinct language encapsulates a world view that is untranslatable. (See Benjamin Whorf, *Four Articles on Metalinguistics* [Washington, D.C., 1949] and also *Language, Thought, and Reality: Selected Writings of Benjamin Lee Whorf*, ed. John B. Carroll [Cambridge, Mass., 1956].) Whorf and the "extreme relativists" who follow him contend

phors implies a fall from truth also. For it is the nature
of metaphor to assume the appearance of the lie, since

---

that the structure of our thought and perception is so radically determined by the structure of our language—that
language is, in neo-Kantian fashion, so constitutive of reality for us—that no genuine understanding is possible
between speakers of different languages. The "limited relativists," on the other hand, acknowledge the powerful influence of language on the world view of its users, but feel
that this makes it only difficult, not impossible, to bridge linguistic gaps.

In these terms, Richard, who feels as bonded to his kingship as his language is to reality, begins as an extreme rela-
tivist and is gradually compelled to abandon this view as he
moves toward verbal anarchy. Of course the difference between Richard and Whorf is that Richard assumes a natural,
inherent, divinely certified bond between his words and
reality, whereas Whorf regards such connections as entirely
arbitrary, varying from language to language. If Whorf
were correct—if we were as thoroughly victimized by linguistic determinism as the extreme relativists argue—new
meanings and concepts would be as impossible to come by
as new kings would be, if Richard's view of kingship prevailed. But Henry IV *is* crowned, and new meanings *are*
created—Shakespeare is creating them himself in the very
process of writing about the uncrowning of a Divine Right
king.

Using Whorf as an analogue here, I should add, is not
wholly anachronistic, since the notion that our view of
reality is prescribed in large part by language has been
around a good while. Indeed, Bacon entertained it in con-
tending that man's warped conceptions of nature in the sixteenth century derived from the linguistic perspectives he
inherited from Aristotelian logic, scholastic theology, and
neoclassic rhetoric. And it was with a vain Whorfian hope
that seventeenth-century linguists sought to create a universal language so structured that men's minds must per-
force see the world as it was scientifically thought to be.

both, as the Houyhnhnms put it, "say the thing that is not."

The linguistic issue is dramatized in terms of the royal "name." In Richard's Divine Right view, "king" is part of his own proper name—inherently legitimate, inviolable, even unquestionable. Usurped by Bolingbroke and applied to himself as "Henry IV," the name of "king" becomes ambiguous—at best, a term abruptly redefined in meaning, at worst, a lie that invades all of the King's English and breaks the bonds of meaning. What, then, of the young Prince Hal, the future king? Applied to the wastrel prince, the title of king must appear a lie too. Or, from the perspective of the tavern world, it must seem a delicious joke whose punch line will burst riotously on England shortly after Hal's coronation.

Hal is himself willing to exploit the appearance of a lie, as his first soliloquy informs us, but in the long run his view of his relation to kingship is metaphoric, and in this regard he distinguishes himself from both Richard and Bolingbroke. For him, the title will no longer possess the Divine Right status of a personal name, as it did for Richard, because he maintains a metaphoric doubleness of focus between vehicle and tenor, name and person, never forgetting that there are ironic distinctions between His Highness Henry the Fifth and the man whom the drawers called "a Corinthian, a lad of mettle, a good boy (by the Lord, so they call me)" (1 *Hen. IV*, 2.4.11–13). If the royal title is not part of his personal name, neither is it merely a piece of stolen property, like "King Henry the Fourth." As with all metaphors, Hal must somehow demonstrate the truth of his kingship in the teeth of his apparent

—in fact, his heir apparent—falseness. For a Divine Right he must substitute an earned human right to the crown. Only then can kingship be invested with meaning.

And Shakespeare? He, no less than Prince Hal, is called in doubt by Bolingbroke's usurpation and the fall of speech. If the king is a lie in the political realm, the lie is now king in the verbal world—and he who practices in that world must needs seem a liar. So the would-be king Hal and the would-be playwright Shakespeare must acknowledge themselves apparent liars to begin with, and somehow wrest truth from that false appearance. Both must transcend Bolingbroke and achieve authentic sovereignty in their separate realms of politics and art.

· 2 ·

Henry IV:

THE ASCENDANCE
OF THE LIE

The shift of power in England from Richard to Boling-broke marks a movement from, among other things, verbal realism to skepticism. The consequences of this movement, which are explored in the remainder of *The Henriad*, involve language not merely as a social instrument within Shakespeare's fictional England but as the literary medium that ministers to the artistic life of the dramatist himself. In what sense does the fall of Richard—and with him the fall of a sacramental language—represent for Shakespeare his own loss of a kind of verbal grace? Obviously Shakespeare did not entertain Richard's naive faith in the absolute equation of word and thing. He knew as well as Bacon that words and things are discrete, and he usually treats the substantive powers of the word lightly. The most famous speech in *Romeo and Juliet* is based on a nominalistic separation of Romeos and roses from the words that so arbitrarily name them. And when Feste in *Twelfth Night* wishes his sister had no name and Viola-Cesario asks "Why, man?" Feste's reply pokes fun at verbal realism: "Why, sir, her name's a word, and to dally with that word might make my sister wanton" (3.1.22–23).

Still, though he surely knew that words are separable from their referents, as in different languages they so obviously become, he also knew that individuals are not free to choose languages. Poets and ordinary citizens alike inherit the King's English by the same process of lineal descent that the king inherits his crown. And with the King's English they inherit a world order. This world order resides primarily in the major metaphors that dominate the language and therefore the consciousness of a society at any point in history. Such metaphors gain in influence as they lose metaphoric status and acquire the literalness and conventional legitimacy of names, becoming objects of unexamined belief, as they are for Richard, as they were for the sixteenth century. With Richard's fall the legitimacy of names falls too. Words that seemed automatically right, even divinely right, are now revealed as metaphors of merely human origin—"idols," in Bacon's term.[1] The world order no longer "named" but

1. In Bacon's theory of idols man's mind, which was capable of a perfect knowledge of nature and the universe before the Fall, no longer serves as a faithful mirror of reality. Even after the Fall man might have regained his purity of intellectual vision through religion and faith, but as Paolo Rossi summarizes Bacon's view—"With sinful arrogance [man] tried to make reality correspond to his assumptions rather than to the stamp set upon it by God. It is these worlds and assumptions that must be destroyed before the mind of man can again reflect reality, and the chaste and holy wedlock of Mind and Universe can be renewed" (*Francis Bacon: From Magic to Science* [Chicago, 1968], p. 163). Bacon classified language among the "idols of the marketplace" and said more specifically: "The idols imposed by words on the understanding are of two kinds. They are either names of things which do not exist . . . ,

only figuratively projected stands in doubt. Like the human mind, human language is an enchanted glass distorting the nature of reality. It is now clear that words have no binding contracts with either their meanings or the truth of the world, but are only tenuously connected by short-term agreements subject, like kingship, to renegotiation on demand.

*

Having reached this point, let us now consider the degraded state in which language finds itself once it passes into Bolingbroke's lax keeping. The financial terms with which I ended the previous section are appropriate because the secularization of politics in *Richard II* and *Henry IV* is paralleled by the commercialization of the word. The sacredness of Richard's

---

or they are names of things which exist but yet confused and ill-defined, and hastily and irregularly derived from realities. Of the first kind are Fortune, the Prime Mover, Planetary Orbits, Element of Fire, and like fictions which owe their origin to false and idle theories" (From *Redargutio philosophiarum*, quoted in Rossi, *Francis Bacon*, p. 171). Names derived from metaphors taken as articles of faith distort man's conception of reality. This was Bacon's preoccupation—how metaphors and other verbal prisms in language affected nature. Shakespeare, though neither metaphysician nor empiricist, also saw language as a means to an end, but the end was art, not nature. A distorting language—language that at bottom rested on a lie—called his art in question no less than it called Bacon's nature in question. Bacon as much as possible scuttled language and went by the route of experiment direct to things, an option hardly open to Shakespeare, who instead put language repeatedly into the crucible of drama to test its temper and truth.

political rule has two sources. It descends from God, as Richard never tires of proclaiming, and it rises from the soil. Of the former, we have said enough. The significance of the latter is underscored by the fact that in John of Gaunt's great rolling lament for a declining England in 2.1, Richard's foulest failing—despite such crimes as Richard's murder of Gloucester, which Gaunt knows about—is reserved, after the tremendous substantive weight of the appositives Gaunt chains together for nineteen lines, for the terse predicate:

> [This royal throne of kings, this sceptred isle, . . .]
> Is now leased out, I die pronouncing it,
> Like to a tenement or pelting farm.
>
> (2.1.59–60)

Richard's most heinous crime—this conversion of his landed wealth into ready capital—reflects the medieval-to-Renaissance shift from agrarianism to mercantilism, from a land-based to a money-based system of economic value. Investing in money value, Richard subjects himself and England to the vagaries of an arbitrary system of worth. The medieval belief in land was "grounded" in the fact that land has intrinsic value, but money, having no intrinsic value of its own, can become valuable only by convention and postulate. The Richard who returns from Ireland to pat the earth, doing it favors with his royal hands after having leased it out to creditors, assumes the automatic inviolability of his ownership no matter what he does. Similarly, he feels that his God-given language as king is intrinsically true and unassailable no matter how whimsically he employs it. Unlike Bolingbroke he fails to realize that the value of his words derives not from divine fiat but from human trust. The king must give his words the stamp of truth no less than he must give his minted coins the stamped image of his face if both are to be honored by his subjects.

Bolingbroke understands that the meaning and value of words are dependent on common acceptance rather than divine backing. Concordantly he understands that a man may buy his way to a throne. Though he returns from France with ironic messianic intentions, expressed in monetary images—he will "Redeem from broking pawn the blemished crown" (2.1.293)—his theft of the crown only blemishes it further. In 1 *Henry IV* Bolingbroke's debts—what he owes his fellow entrepreneurs for investing in his kingship and what he owes God and the nation for his murder of Richard —are called in, but to no avail. With speech degenerated to the status of money, Bolingbroke's verbal exchequer contains nothing but unredeemed promissory notes. The kingly word that ought to unite the nation by proving truly redemptive cannot keep its own promises, such as that of making the pilgrimage to the Holy Land, or ransom back the captured Mortimer, a pretender to the throne. Even when Bolingbroke offers to pay off "with interest" before Shrewsbury (4.3.49), Hotspur is suspicious:

> well we know the King
> Knows at what time to promise, when to pay.
> (lines 52–53)

It is for fear that the older conspirators "shall pay for all" (5.2.23) that Worcester intercepts and perverts Bolingbroke's one word of mercy before it can reach Hotspur's ears.

The Ascendance of the Lie

On the battlefield at Shrewsbury the man whose kingship is a lie is fittingly unrecognizable to Douglas:

> What art thou
> That counterfeit'st the person of a king?
>
> (5.4.27–28)

> I fear thou art another counterfeit.
>
> (5.4.35)

With no divine treasury backing up Henry's verbal currency, the kingly word is as counterfeit as the kingly person. And so as we turn to 2 *Henry IV* it is not God or the divinely inspired Word in the mouth of an anointed king that binds the English together in Gaunt's lost paradise, "This blessed plot, this earth, this realm, this England." Instead, it is Rumor, "painted full of tongues" (Induction). Rumor, the counterfeit word—

> The which in every language I pronounce,
> Stuffing the ears of men with false reports
>
> (Ind., lines 7–8)

—runs whispering the length and breadth of England uniting the nation in a lie, a "black mass" travesty of the political "communion" that language seeks to create.

With Rumor presiding over 2 *Henry IV*, the lie has reached its ascendancy. At Gaultree Forest the lie becomes the instrument of official policy as Prince John's betrayal of the rebels is explicitly dramatized in terms of the unredeemed word:

Archbishop. I take your princely word for these addresses.

Lancaster.	I give it you and will maintain my word. . . .
	The word of peace is rendered.
	(4.2.66–67, 87)

To make it clear that this is not merely the random deviousness of one individual but symbolic of English authority itself, Shakespeare must revise Holinshed, converting Prince John from the mute bystander he was in the *Chronicles*, where Westmoreland was in charge, to chief negotiator and official spokesman for Henry IV. The rebels surrender in good faith to this unregal lie, just as Colville of the Dale surrenders in the following scene to Falstaff, the walking lie, counterfeit killer of Hotspur.

God has not been allowed to speak since the opening of *Richard II* when Richard, preventing the trial by combat between Mowbray and Bolingbroke, substituted his own sentence of exile for what was to have been God's judgment. It is in keeping with the secularizing of kingship that after Shrewsbury there should be no references to God's having supplied militant angels to defend His, in this case, unanointed king. But by the time we reach Gaultree Forest things have declined to the point where Prince John's machinations are blandly passed off as God's verdict in behalf of Henry: "God, and not we," John says, "hath safely fought today" (4.2.121). Much virtue in that "safely"![2]

2. On this piece of princely chicanery Sigurd Burckhardt offers some typically perceptive observations emphasizing the secularizing of kingship and, from a formal standpoint, indicating how this unchivalric resolution of rebellion defeats our expectations (*Shakespearean Meanings* [Princeton, 1968], pp. 149–156).

John's conduct at Gaultree Forest is both an illustrative corollary to Shakespeare's rumor-ridden Induction and a gloss on Henry's later death. If Rumor is the emblem of an England ruled by the lie and peacefully united only by falsehood—

> I speak of peace, while covert enmity
> Under the smile of safety wounds the world
> $\qquad$ (Ind., lines 9–10)

—Prince John at Gaultree Forest literalizes that emblem. "Literal" is the word for John in another sense too, for when rebuked by the Archbishop for breaking his faith, he relies on a most literal interpretation of his words to deny the facts. He promised redress of certain grievances, he says, and will in good faith keep his promise—as for executing rebels, that is of course another matter. That fair is foul, John paltering with words in a typically Lancastrian double sense, seems instantly evident to Henry, whose guilt invades him physically the moment he learns of Gaultree. "And wherefore should these good news make me sick?" he asks, and wonders why Fortune writes "her fair words still in foulest letters" (4.4.102–104).

Henry, like John, has found equivocation a device of much virtue. In 3.1 he recites to Warwick the official version of his usurpation, the version he acted out for all his fellow conspirators in *Richard II*—

> Though then, God knows, I had no such intent,
> But that necessity so bowed the state
> That I and greatness were compelled to kiss
> $\qquad$ (lines 72–74)

—but to Prince Hal he tells another tale, one that is endowed with the conventional deathbed veracity:

Henry IV

> God knows, my son,
> By what by-paths and indirect crooked ways
> I met this crown.
>
> (4.5.184–186)

The lie that appears as a literal truth, a truth in name only, as Henry has been a king in name only, repeats itself in the king's deathbed pilgrimage to Jerusalem. Henry has just explained to Hal that the high spiritual aim of his long postponed pilgrimage was but window-dressing for a low political stratagem; his intent was not so much to do penance for Richard's murder as—

> To lead out many to the Holy Land,
> Lest rest and lying still might make them look
> Too near unto my state.
>
> (4.5.211–213)

In the reciprocities of history, one profaned word and unredeemed promise, it seems, merits another, and so Henry's pilgrimage ends, if not spiritually in the Holy Land, literally in the "Jerusalem chamber" at Westminster. As he was king in name only, so he is saved in name only, happily exclaiming in his moral obtuseness "Laud be to God!"

*

In Henry and his pupil John, and in the figure of Rumor, Shakespeare plays out the consequences of linguistic debasement in England. With the legitimacy of the word brought low and the lie in pride of place, not only kingship and power but words as well are up for grabs, much as Shakespeare phrased it in *Sir Thomas More* when More warns the rebellious mob that order once fallen is down for good:

38

For other ruffians, as their fancies wrought,
With self-same hand, self reasons, and self right,
Would shark on you, and men, like ravenous fishes,
Would feed on one another.

This should remind us that we have not yet dealt with another ruffian with a sharkish appetite, if not shape: "If the young dace be a bait for the old pike, I see no reason in the law of nature but I may snap at him" (2 *Hen. IV*, 3.2.355–357). Once true legitimacy and authority are gone, anything is possible, even Sir John Falstaff. There is no room in the world of Richard II for Falstaff; Bolingbroke must sweep the way before him. King Henry enfranchises Sir John.

Falstaff needs no instruction in verbal skepticism. He knows instinctively that words can be turned inside out like cheveril gloves and that all large ideals have small cash value. Honor, for instance?

Sir Walter Blunt. There's honor for you.
(I *Hen. IV*, 5.3.32)

Military glory and patriotism?

Tut, tut, good enough to toss. Food for powder, food for powder; they'll fill a pit as well as better. Tush, man, mortal men, mortal men.
(1 *Hen. IV*, 4.2.71–74)

Truth?

There is Percy. If your father will do me any honor, so. If not, let him kill the next Percy himself. I look to be either earl or duke, I assure you.
(1 *Hen. IV*, 5.4.143–145)

The concept of order in man and society, the cherished notion of man the microcosm whose "spirit" reflects divinity?

It [sherris] illumineth the face, which as a beacon
gives warning to all the rest of this little kingdom,
man, to arm. And then the vital commoners and
inland petty spirits muster me all to their captain,
the heart, who, great and puffed up with this reti-
nue, doth any deed of courage.

(2 *Hen. IV*, 4.3.115–121)

Like Bolingbroke forcing the celestial Richard down
into the base court at Flint Castle, Falstaff reduces all
values to their lowest level of humorous construction
and finds there no great matter. All are merely versions
of a central official lie designed, rather like the Tudor
homilies, to maintain order and keep the Establishment
in power. The biggest lie of all is one of the keystones
of political order, the notion of the true anointed king
set apart from his lesser fellows by divine distinction,
which becomes for Falstaff the fictitious stuffing for a
self-exonerating jibe:

By the Lord, I knew ye as well as he that made ye.
Why, hear you, my masters—was it for me to
kill the heir apparent? Should I turn upon the true
prince? Why, thou knowest I am as valiant as
Hercules—but beware instinct! The lion will not
touch the true prince. Instinct is a great matter. I
was now a coward on instinct. I shall think the
better of myself and thee during my life—I for a
valiant lion and thou for a true prince.

(1 *Hen. IV*, 2.4.294–303)

With all values reduced to absurdity, what remains
is simply survival in a sea full of daces and old pikes.
If Bolingbroke improvised his way to the crown, Falstaff, going his monarch one better, improvises to survive. That he literally lives by improvisation is graph-

ically illustrated at Shrewsbury when he finds himself
unexpectedly playing the dace to Douglas's not so old
but exceedingly voracious pike: "Sblood! 'Twas time
to counterfeit, or that hot termagant Scot had paid me
scot and lot too!" (5.4.113–115). Improvisation is necessarily a mode of the moment, which is why Hal
replies to Falstaff's first words with—

> What a devil hast thou to do with the time of day?
> Unless hours were cups of sack, and minutes ca-
> pons, and clocks the tongues of bawds, and dials
> the signs of leaping-houses, and the blessed sun
> himself a fair hot wench in flame-colored taffeta,
> I see no reason why thou shouldest be so super-
> fluous to demand the time of the day.
>
> (1 Hen. IV, 1.2.6–13)

Reality for Falstaff is portioned out in a succession of
lean present-tense slices, with one exception: his casting his expectations forward to that vague point in the
future when with Hal as king he need improvise no
longer, when the minute-by-minute scramble for sack
and capons will turn magically into an eternal banquet.
But apart from this dream vision he abandons the future to its own devices, appropriately denying the advance of time, as an unhistorical character in a history
play should, while living in an eternal present of sensual indulgence: "Hostess, clap to the doors. Watch
tonight, pray tomorrow!" (2.4.305)

Falstaff appears to bespeak an old tendency toward
sensual verbal indulgence in Shakespeare, a tendency
that he has been punishing and symbolically killing
off—or at least badly wounding—throughout a series
of early plays, most recently in *Richard II*. There is

much to be said for this. What was earlier a lyric self-indulgence on Shakespeare's part, a playful poetic interest in words for their own supple sakes and a tardiness in getting on with the action of the play, seems now to have corporealized itself in the suety shape of Falstaff. As wordplay in general involves a densening of the phonic substance of speech, so Falstaff the verbal improviser and embodiment of language games represents the full fleshing out of the word.[3] He has been at a great feast of languages and has fed well on epithets, puns, sententia, inkhorn terms, bombast, slang, and all manner of styles from the biblical to the euphuistic to the mock-heroic to the fishwife screech. He seems almost to have swallowed the whole text of *Love's Labour's Lost*. So surfeit swelled with words, he bestrides the path of dramatic action in *Henry IV* like a colossus —or would do so if he were allowed on that path.

But Shakespeare, who is sufficiently cavalier with history to invent Falstaff in the first place and give him such prominence, is true to time at least in this: within the two plays he relegates Falstaff to a side-

3. In "Ceremony and History: The Problem of Symbol from *Richard II* to *Henry V*," in *Pacific Coast Studies in Shakespeare*, ed. Waldo F. McNeir and Thelma N. Greenfield, (Eugene, Ore., 1966), Eric LaGuardia shrewdly observes of Falstaff that "In his massive corporeality, it would seem, the word resides. He becomes by virtue of being the source of all invention, the ironic incarnation of the possibilities of language" (pp. 81–82). My own notion of Falstaff as corporealized word derives from ideas about the substantializing of language in wordplay, an issue that gets bruited about in my *Shakespearean Metadrama* (Minneapolis, Minn., 1971), particularly in the chapter on *Love's Labour's Lost*.

world, or a side-board, boxed off from recorded doings. Falstaff is to history as Academe and the Capulets' orchard are to the extramural world of affairs in those plays. It is not of course that Falstaff never acts but simply that his actions are not allowed to intrude into history. The one claim he makes to affect history—his "killing" of Hotspur—must of necessity be a lie; and it is precisely when he attempts to insert himself into history, at Hal's coronation, that he must be rejected. (Of this, more later in subsequent chapters.)

So Falstaff, who feeds on language no less than on capons and sack, who appropriates the word for his own lying uses, seems a perfect embodiment, a final profane reincarnation of Shakespeare's impulse to create verbal worlds sufficient unto themselves, self-contained, self-absorbed, outside and largely indifferent to the mainstream of dramatic action. So stuffed with speech is he that doing is beyond him, he can only *be* —for there is an inevitable inertia to the word in itself as opposed to the inherently kinetic thrust of action. Not that Falstaff cherishes words for their own aesthetic selves. On the contrary, he is the "user" of words par excellence. But he uses them as his body does sack and capons. Through the metabolism of his wit they are transformed into the lying instruments of his most immediate corporeal needs. As an inveterate improviser Falstaff can use words only in the present; he cannot enlist them in the service of future action. He has no plans or programs. In short, he cannot plot, he can only extemporize to evade the plots of others, like Hal and Poins, or simply those of the world at large, which from his point of view seems increasingly ill-disposed toward white-haired old knights scoured almost to nothing with perpetual motion in behalf of the state.

Given all this, then, how has Shakespeare profited from his earlier dramatic efforts? Is he not merely wantoning again, or this time roistering, with words at the expense of action and plot—and indeed doing it so hilariously well that Falstaff is in danger of swallowing up the play much as the word-games did in *Love's Labour's Lost* (so that in 2 *Henry IV* Shakespeare must have Hal play Mercade and dismiss the holiday of words in favor of an everyday of history)? Well, there is, as I've said, much to support such a view, and in later chapters I shall try to talk along these lines. But from another standpoint Shakespeare's treatment of Falstaff represents an advance upon his treatment of the scholars of Navarre, the lovers of Verona, or the late English king. For while Falstaff is using the word for his short-range selfish purposes Shakespeare is using Falstaff for his long-range artistic ones. That is, though Falstaff is isolated from the history plot in terms of action, he nevertheless participates in it verbally because his words reveal him to us as a burlesque low-life metaphor for Henry IV.

This point is a familiar one and needs no laboring here. Psychoanalytic critics like J. I. M. Stewart and Ernst Kris began seeing Falstaff as a father-substitute —a sacrificial stand-in for Bolingbroke—years ago.[4] What needs stressing here is not the fact of Falstaffian burlesque but its relevance to the linguistic issues discussed earlier. Shakespeare's use of Falstaff as a

4. J. I. M. Stewart, *Character and Motive in Shakespeare* (London, 1949) and Ernst Kris, *Psychoanalytic Explorations in Art* (New York, 1952).

metaphor for the king follows logically from his having dramatized in *Richard II* the discovery of the metaphor within the name. Moreover, it is by means of metaphor that the word emerges from isolation and comes into its dramatic own. In its very doubleness of focus, that is, metaphor enables the word to reach beyond itself to engage with actions elsewhere, so that Falstaff need not lumber bodily into the main historical plot in order to play a part in it. Merely by heaving himself onto his joint-stool throne in the kingdom of the Boar's Head Tavern, fisting his leaden-dagger sceptre, and commencing in his King Cambyses tone, "Harry, I do not only marvel where thou spendest thy time" (1 *Hen. IV*, 2.4.439), Falstaff casts his broad shadow of verbal parody forward into 3.2 of the main plot where Henry—pompous as Falstaff in his regal mood and rendered complacently tutorial by the success of his self-serving political strategies ("Thus did I keep my person fresh and new, / My presence, like a robe pontifical, / Ne'er seen but wondered at" etc.)—reveals himself to be as much a self-constituted, play-acting, inauthentic monarch as his bombastic low-life counterpart. To Hal's scornful critique of Falstaff's performance—"Dost thou speak like a king?" (2.4.476)—Falstaff's answer might well be "As much like a king as Bolingbroke, and with as much legal justification."

In 1 *Henry IV*, then, it is not Falstaff who plays the role of Richard II—the role of the man whose poetic speech makes direct claims on the world but proves powerless in the event. That role devolves on Glendower, the poet-seer who issues commands to the devil and calls spirits from the vasty deep but who cannot liberate himself, in Hotspur's derisive view, from the categories of liar and pompous ass. Shakespeare is well beyond Richard now, and beyond poetic isolation. His concern is with the political word and how it makes its way in the world of action and history where Glendower, secluded in Wales and rapt in private dreams and prophecies that warn him away from history, never ventures.

If Falstaff ventures not directly but metaphorically into history, into the world of Henry IV, by becoming a burlesque version of kingship himself, that may strike a blow for metaphor but it also raises questions about kingship. If Bolingbroke is a false king, a lie, and Falstaff is a burlesque king, a metaphor, where does true kingship reside? Can there be a species of truth in lies and metaphors? These are questions to which the heir apparent, the young Prince Hal, must address himself as he makes his own indirect, if not crooked, way to the throne.

Henry IV:

COUNTERFEIT KINGS AND
CREATIVE SUCCESSION

At the battle of Shrewsbury Field the ferocious but somewhat befuddled Douglas discovers a superabundance of kings, or at least of kingly clothes, for "The King," as Hotspur informs him, "hath many marching in his coats" (5.3.25). Not gifted with Falstaff's unerring instinct for registering the presence of the true prince, Douglas must resort to trial-and-error empiricism:

> Now, by my sword, I will kill all his coats.
> I'll murder all his wardrobe, piece by piece.
> Until I meet the king.
> (1 Hen. IV, 5.3.26–28)

Douglas's problem is more difficult than it seems. When he has done away with the Lord of Stafford, coat and all, he comes to Sir Walter Blunt and is told that this time he faces the true king. Sir Walter in his turn goes to it, and the disgusted Douglas, on learning of his mistake, says:

> A borrowed title hast thou bought too dear.
> Why didst thou tell me that thou wert a king?
> (5.3.23–24)

Since Henry has possessed himself of a "borrowed title" also—for which he too has paid dearly, though not so dearly as Richard II or Sir Walter—there is much reason in Douglas's doubts when he encounters him:

> What art thou,
> That counterfeit'st the person of a king?
> *Henry.* The King himself . . .
> *Doug.* I fear thou art another counterfeit.
> (5.4.27–35)

Once the identity of the king is no longer certified by divine authority, any man may march in a royal coat. Kingly trappings such as crown, throne, and vestments must substitute for congenital royalty as a guide to the king's person.

Moreover, not all those who can lay some claim to kingship are marching in the king's coats at Shrewsbury Field. In the first place, one of them can not march very far on any field and could hardly get into the king's tent, let alone his coat. Yet at the end of the last chapter we saw that Falstaff, King of Misrule, could counterfeit Henry IV in the suspenseful dramas staged by the Boar's Head Inn players. For that matter—after the deposition of Falstaff—so could Hal, rehearsing for realities to come. And according to Douglas there is still another pretender to royalty—Hotspur, "the king of honour" (4.1.10), whose favorite horse is appropriately his "throne" (2.3.73). Henry himself has called our attention to Hotspur as a potential king when he upbraided Hal in 3.2:

> Now, by my sceptre and my soul to boot,
> He hath more worthy interest to the state

48

Than thou, the shadow of succession.
(lines 97–99)

If Falstaff is, as critics have suggested, a father-substitute, and hence a king-substitute, then Hotspur is a son-substitute, and hence a figurative heir apparent, a king in potentia.

Thus the striking picture of Douglas roaming Shrewsbury Field murdering wardrobes in hope of finding a king in the flesh as well as in the coat, this stress on royal counterfeits not merely reinforces the fact that Bolingbroke is prudentially devious, which we have known for a good while anyhow. Nor does it only reemphasize the spuriousness of Bolingbroke's title, which makes him indistinguishable from other counterfeit kings. It also emphasizes a situation not limited to the battlefield but pervasive throughout the play: the disappearance of authentic kingship among a host of counterfeits.

With the collapse of a language founded on names —a language in which words are true designators bonded firmly to the world of things, as the name of king seemed bonded to Richard—all language must henceforth appear a collective lie, and all kings counterfeit. If true authority and kingship have not permanently disappeared with Richard's death, they have at least receded into conceptual vagueness—an unexampled ideal and abstract mystery. Since abstractions can be apprehended only indirectly, through metaphor,[1] we

1. We can never satisfactorily conceive of abstractions like *being, justice, relation, situation,* by approaching them on their own terms, abstractly. That is what dictionary definitions seek to do as they send us back and forth inside a closed system of abstract reference: *being* means *existence*

are presented in *Henry IV* with four metaphoric versions of kingship: the nominal King of England, the abdominal King of Misrule, the chivalric King of Honor, and the wastrel heir apparent. Or *are* they metaphoric? As we mentioned earlier it is part of the disarming nature of metaphor to march in the coat of the lie and to be identifiable only after a slaughter of wardrobes. For, like Bolingbroke, the metaphor and the lie are usurpers. They confiscate the names that rightfully belong to other concepts. But whereas the stealthy theft of names by the lie impoverishes reality and truth, it is only by means of such a theft, conducted openly by metaphor, that abstract realities and truths can be possessed at all. The trick is in knowing which is which, and it is a trick worthy of a prince's study:

> The Prince but studies his companions
> Like a strange tongue, wherein, to gain the language,
> 'Tis needful that the most immodest word
> Be looked upon and learned; which once attained,
> Your Highness knows, comes to no further use
> But to be known and hated. So, like gross terms,
> The Prince will in the perfectness of time
> Cast off his followers. And their memory
> Shall as a pattern or a measure live,

which means *having actuality* which means *being,* and so on. So we metaphorize, taking a detour through the concrete. Though we tend to think of poets as being in flight from abstractions, they are not; a language full of concrete metaphors is itself an index of the poet's concern with abstractions, because metaphor is the only way in which abstractions may be made intellectually accessible—which is why most abstract words are crystallized metaphors.

By which his Grace must mete the lives of others,
Turning past evils to advantages.
                                        (2 *Hen. IV*, 4.4.68–77)

Warwick speaks truer than he realizes, for Prince Hal's
vocabulary study extends beyond his rowdy followers.
As the heir apparent in search of true kingship, Hal
addresses himself to Bolingbroke, Falstaff, and Hotspur, the pretenders to kingship, as though they were
words which he must study to determine whether each
is a lie—a total counterfeit—or a metaphor containing
a certain kingly truth. In the course of the two plays he
imitates Douglas searching through counterfeits for the
true king.

    Warwick's speech should remind us of Hal's first
soliloquy, his address to the audience in 1 *Henry IV* on
the theme of turning evils to advantages, and especially
of the passage in which Hal refers to his future reformation as a transcending of his word:

So when this loose behaviour I throw off
And pay the debt I never promised,
By how much better than my word I am,
By so much shall I falsify men's hopes.
                                        (1.2.231–234)

The soliloquy as a whole suggests certain connections
between Hal and not only Falstaff but Shakespeare too.
It may be Falstaff who says in 2 *Henry IV* that "A good
wit will make use of anything, I will turn diseases to
commodity" (1.2. 276–278) and who then tries to make
financial use of Shallow—as he has sought all along to
make use of Hal—but in the soliloquy it is Hal who
reveals himself as the man whose wit will make use of

anything or anyone. He conceives here of a sophisticated version of Falstaff's world of pikes preying on
daces. What Falstaff does not realize is that the princely
dace he has been trailing around has, on closer inspec-
tion, a distinctly pike-like and snappish look to him.
Unlike Falstaff, whose specialty is improvisation to sat-
isfy present needs, Hal is capable of long-range calcu-
lations to secure the future. Indeed, as he presents himself here, Hal is a master plotter, a princely dramatist
in whose political drama Falstaff and company are to
play an unwitting role. Hal's drama is a history play in
the comic/heroic mode, featuring the radiant emer-
gence of the true king by means of a sudden peripeteia
that brings the national audience of Englishmen to its
feet united in patriotic feeling.

From the standpoint of language as well as that
of plotting, Hal is an "interior" version of Shakespeare
the controlling playwright. Whereas Falstaff is a walking hyperbole, the man whose speech dwarfs his performances, Hal is the embodiment of meiosis, the man
whose deeds will as he says prove him "better than
[his] word." As it stands, his word is very much in
need of redemptive bettering, for as the instrument by
which he will "falsify men's hopes" it is nothing less
than a lie. And this too he shares with Shakespeare.
Hal begins his "interior drama" as Shakespeare begins
Henry IV, with a fallen language whose lack of inherent truth is emblemized in the lie. But as his soliloquy
indicates, Hal is prepared to use the lie rather than wilt
before it as Richard did. After all, he who uses Falstaff
must by definition use the lie. But also, by creating from
the false image of the wastrel prince a true symbol of
English kingship, Hal will incorporate the lie into a

constructive political program, a drama of skillful offence "redeeming time when men least think [he] will" (1.2.240). And that is Shakespeare's artistic goal as well—to wrest truth from a language devoid of divine or natural authority, to shape from the unseemly material of the lie an authentic order and meaning. No less than Hal, Shakespeare must turn past evils to advantages and prove better than his words.

*

It appears as we move from *Richard II* into *Henry IV* that the lie and the metaphor are the joint consequence of the collapse of a language of names. If so, it is not by accident that both verbal forms abound in *Henry IV*. Not of course that earlier Shakespearean plays are devoid of lies and metaphors but that lie and metaphor do not in themselves rise to thematic prominence or become incorporated into a metadramatic development. Perhaps it is worth noting that even the word *lie* appears far more often now than in earlier plays—twice as often in 1 *Henry IV*, for instance, as in a lie-fraught play like *Richard III*. As for metaphor, how deeply Shakespeare's imagination has delved in figuration in these plays needs little documentation at this late date. Working chronologically through the early plays, and especially through the histories, one is taken aback by the sudden plenitude of comparatives, analogues, parallels, versions, and similitudes in *Henry IV*—all the vast network of metaphoric association by which everything appears in the likeness of something else. With characters, actions, and images multiplying with the spontaneous fertility of Falstaff's men in buckram, we may despair of isolating any one feature of the play for consideration, and despair no less of encompassing the whole. But because it figures in Hal's quest for true kingship among various usurping counterfeits, let me linger a bit over Shakespeare's metaphoric employment of the double plot.

That double plots may be structural metaphors is perhaps most obvious in *The Merchant of Venice*, where by playing Belmont off against Venice Shakespeare dramatizes the metaphor "love is a form of commerce," or in *Troilus and Cressida*, where the two plots embody the metaphor "love is a form of war."[2] In similar fashion 2 *Henry IV* places the major actions of the historical and the nonhistorical plot in metaphoric juxtaposition to dramatize the notion that "Shrewsbury is a form of Gadshill," which suggests that the English rebels are merely history's cutpurses— as anxious to split their take in English soil (see 3.1.70–141) as Falstaff's "gentlemen of the shade" are their liberated gold—and that the two great leaders, Falstaff and Hotspur, may have a kind of half-faced fellowship despite vast differences.

More important in light of Prince Hal's search for kingship is the fact that at Gadshill and Shrewsbury the heir apparent both protects a crown and seizes a crown. What is being robbed at Gadshill is in large part Henry himself—"There's money of the King's coming down the hill; 'tis going to the King's exchequer" (2.2.56–57)—and what is stolen is pointedly associated with the royal symbol of office, the crown, as in Poins's invitation, "If you will go, I will stuff your purses full of crowns" (1.2.145–146). In low-life

2. In *Some Versions of Pastoral* (London, 1935), William Empson analyses double plots along these lines (pp. 25–84).

metaphor Falstaff, by stealing crowns from the royal exchequer, usurps Henry's crown and so becomes a mock-king, as befits a King of Misrule. And Falstaff suffers from Henry's royal ailment also—a reign marked by internal dissension. After a brief but heroic skirmish against armies of rebellious knaves in Kendall green and buckram, Falstaff is "uncrowned" by Hal, who subsequently restores the crowns/crown to the dispossessed Henry ("The money is paid back again," 3.3.200). Later in the Boar's Head Tavern, Hal uncrowns Falstaff twice more, once metaphorically when he makes the master of humor the butt of the whole joke and once theatrically when he demotes him from a kingly to a merely princely role:

> *Prince.* Dost thou speak like a king? Do thou stand for me, and I'll play my father.
> *Falstaff.* Depose me? If thou dost it half so gravely, so majestically, both in word and matter, hang me up by the heels for a rabbit-sucker or a poulter's hare.
>
> (2.4.476–481)

At the battle of Shrewsbury Field the metaphors of robbery, crowns, and kingly coinage are convened again. Douglas, fighting his way from one counterfeit king to another, finally locates Henry and comes dangerously near seizing his life and crown before his robbery is prevented by Hal, "Who never promiseth but he means to pay" (5.4.43). The major highwayman in the rebel company, however, is Hotspur, who has spent an almost furiously busy life relieving chivalric travelers of their martial reputations. His roadside cry is not Falstaff's "Your money or your life" but "Your

55

honors and your life." On the one hand, as leader of the rebels at Shrewsbury, Hotspur is in the role of robber attempting to seize Henry's life, land, and crown, which Henry has of course robbed from Richard. At the same time Hotspur is himself the victim of a robbery. In this role he is, in Douglas's phrase, the "king of honor" and is concerned to retain his title despite the challenge of Hal. Thus their encounter is figured as a contest for a crown, as in Hal's baiting remarks on their dual sovereignty:

> I am the Prince of Wales; and think not, Percy,
> To share with me in glory any more.
> Two stars keep not their motion in one sphere,
> Nor can one England brook a double reign
> Of Harry Percy and the Prince of Wales.
> (5.4.63–67)

Hal's uncrowning of Percy is suggestive of Bolingbroke's uncrowning of Richard. Henry himself a bit earlier had claimed that history was about to repeat itself, but in rebuking Hal for bad conduct he put him and Hotspur in the wrong roles:

> For all the world
> As thou art to this hour was Richard then
> When I from France set foot at Ravenspurgh,
> And even as I was then is Percy now.
> (3.2.93–96)

In fact, of course, Hal the careful plotter and manipulator of his followers has been very much his father's son; and Percy, despite his un-Ricardian life of action, has been like Richard in that for him the split in speech, the breakdown of a monistic language of names, has never occurred. Hotspur still lives in a world in which honor, Esperance, and truth have real and substantial being and in which a man's name or reputation is a possession as dear as life itself.

Percy's defeat at the hands of Hal, then, is appropriately a usurpation of "name." Like his father coming ashore at Ravenspurgh, Hal is essentially nameless compared to Hotspur, who complains, as titled champions will, of having nothing to win and everything to lose:

> and would to God
> Thy name in arms were now as great as mine.
> (5.4.69–70)

Thus when Hotspur dies it is not the loss of "brittle life" but the loss of "those proud titles thou hast won of me" that grieves him deepest (5.4.78–79), which might remind us of Richard's loss of identity and his sense of personal emptiness once he is deprived of his kingly name (*Rich. II*, 4.1.255–262). That emptiness is a measure also of the Hotspur code of value, and the question of the Shrewsbury moment is whether in conquering the King of Honor Hal has not only taken Hotspur's crown but adopted his limited moral vision as part of the spoils too.

That Hal might not only defeat but in a sense become Hotspur seemed a real danger when, in his interview earlier with his disapproving father, he spoke of redeeming his sorry reputation:

> Percy is but my factor, good my lord,
> To engross up glorious deeds on my behalf.
> And I will call him to so strict account

That he shall render every glory up,
Yea, even the slightest worship of his time,
Or I will tear the reckoning from his heart.
(1 *Hen. IV*, 3.3.148–152)

Here Hal translates Falstaff's world of daces and pursuing pikes into financial terms. Falstaff collects purses, Hotspur collects titles of honor, and Hal—a princely internal revenue service—collects from both. But whereas Hal has earlier been capable of registering amusement at the extravagant self-absorption of Hotspur's code of honor (2.4.113–125), in his remarks now to his father and again to Percy just before they fight it does not seem apparent to Hal that all he can collect from Percy are counterfeit "crowns."

But the Gadshill parallel holds true in the event. Just as Hal transcended Falstaff's pursetaking by returning the Gadshill money to the king's exchequer, so now, after Hotspur's death, he transcends Hotspur's obsession with names and titles of honor not only by surrendering his rightful earnings to the old horseback-breaking highwayman himself—

There is Percy. If your father will do me any honour,
so. If not, let him kill the next Percy himself. I
look to be either earl or duke, I can assure you.
(5.4.143–146)

—but by even contributing amusedly to the thievery:

For my part, if a lie may do thee grace,
I'll gild it with the happiest terms I have.
(5.4.161–162)

In so doing he earns title to a far more impressive kingship than any of the pseudo-versions put before him throughout the play.

And yet Hal registers in each of these counterfeit kingships a certain metaphoric truth in the process of transcending them, collecting something from each as he prepares to pay England the debt he never promised. His most glorious payment to England occurs at Agincourt, where all debts come due, and it is there that his "factors" Falstaff and Hotspur pay off for him as well. Without expatiating on the kingly and human lessons Hal learns from the men he has uncrowned—an old theme—we can merely observe that his easy way with men, which is summed up on the eve of battle by the choral phrase "A little touch of Harry in the night," is as inconceivable without Falstaff and Gadshill as his rallying Saint Crispian speech, with its "But if it be a sin to covet honour / I am the most offending soul alive" (*Hen. V*, 4.3.28–29), is without Hotspur and Shrewsbury.[3]

*

At Gadshill and Shrewsbury Prince Hal defeats Falstaff and Hotspur on their own terms, stealing a laugh from the one, a life from the other, and a metaphoric crown from both. There remains in the plays a final version of kingship—the king himself. If we wonder what metaphoric truths Hal discovers in Henry or

3. I should add here that Hal's covetousness about honor—his claim not to want an additional soldier present because he can't bear to divide up the glories of the coming day—is quite a different thing from Hotspur's refusal to await reinforcements at Shrewsbury in favor of a "Die all, die merrily" policy. At Agincourt there are no reinforcements to wait for, so Hal makes the rhetorical and military most of what he's got, adopting the Hotspur mode because, given the situation, none other is available.

what debts he collects from him, we are obliged to consider the deathbed scene in 2 *Henry IV* (4.5), for it is here that Hal uncrowns Henry. Both men give and receive. With Henry's apparent death, Hal picks up what is owing him, the crown, and relinquishes what he has long owed Henry, the tears of genuine personal feeling:

> Thy due from me
> Is tears and heavy sorrows of the blood,
> Which nature, love, and filial tenderness
> Shall, O dear father, pay thee plenteously.
> My due from thee is this imperial crown,
> Which, as immediate from thy place and blood,
> Derives itself to me.
>
> (4.5.37–43)

Like Falstaff and Hotspur, Henry it appears is also Hal's factor, to engross up not easy ways or glorious deeds but that one indispensable possession of a king, the crown itself. Not that Hal has hungered for power —but even so, no heir apparent is unconscious of what he is heir to (as Hal has made clear since his first soliloquy). At any rate, when Henry has an untimely recovery, Hal finds himself in a most unpleasant, even Falstaffian situation.

Standing before Henry, crown in hand, Hal appears in the likeness of the one-time tutor and feeder of his riots, Falstaff himself, who was always quick to seize crowns going to or from the king's exchequer. He must also call to mind Hotspur, whose Shrewsbury exploits, had they proved successful, would have uncrowned Henry before his time. Finally and most significantly, Hal must remind us of Bolingbroke himself, who "met this crown," he is shortly to tell Hal, by "indirect crooked ways" (4.5.185–186). But if Hal's apparent theft of the crown raises the image of usurpation, Shakespeare's intention is to suggest a likeness in order to point a difference. Unlike all the counterfeit kings, who in their various fashions are or would be usurpers, "player kings," Hal is not feigning kingship. The role of the man cultivating kingly virtues he has deliberately avoided playing; he has not coveted the crown and pretended otherwise:

> if I do feign,
> O let me in my present wilderness die
> And never live to show the incredulous world
> The noble change that I have purposed!
> (4.5.152–155)[4]

And unlike Hotspur and especially Henry himself, Hal has not contended *for* the crown. He has raised no armies against England's monarch, sent no soldiers to their deaths, killed no king. His only contest is *with* the crown, a private inquiry and test of merit:

> Thus, my most royal liege,
> Accusing it, I put it on my head,
> To try with it, as with an enemy
> That had before my face murdered my father,
> The quarrel of a true inheritor.
> (4.5.165–169)

That Hal's contest with the crown is only a metaphoric battle, the "quarrel of a true inheritor" instead of the ambitious struggles of a usurper, is owing to

4. The word *feign* here carries the meaning both of "act" or "deceive" and, in homonymic pun, "crave." The First Folio spelling, incidentally, is "faine." Thus, on the one hand, "if I do merely 'act' contrite" and, on the other, "if I do actually covet the crown" then "let me die."

61

Henry himself. To Richard II, despite all his keening over it, the crown was essentially an irrelevant possession. Symbols of kingship confer nothing on one who so luminously and infallibly is king, who has been king from birth, and who is descended from a line of kings. For Bolingbroke, possession of the crown is another matter; the symbols of kingship are his only identifying marks. Having killed a king to gain a crown, Bolingbroke has spent a restive reign suffering from the guilt of his possession and from the fear of dispossession—even down to this final moment. But what was a piece of stolen property in Henry's hands is modified by its transfer to his son:

> To thee it shall descend with better quiet,
> Better opinion, better confirmation,
> For all the soil of the achievement goes
> With me into the earth. *It seemed in me*
> *But as an honour snatched with boistrous hand.*
> And I had many living to upbraid
> My gain of it by their assistances,
> Which daily grew to quarrel and to bloodshed,
> Wounding supposed peace. All these bold fears
> Thou see'st with peril I have answered—
> For all my reign hath been but as a scene
> Acting that argument, and now my death
> Changes the mode. For what in me was purchased
> Falls upon thee in a more fairer sort,
> *So thou the garland wear'st successively.*
>
> (4.5.188–202; my italics)

The major function of this scene is to present us with a transfer of the crown from Henry to Hal that is made to look like an act of usurpation, a theft—

Thou hast stolen that which after some few hours
Were thine without offence

(4.5.102–103)

—but that, upon reinterpretation, is seen to be a matter of direct lineal descent. After Hal exonerates himself, both he and Henry recognize that the kingship Bolingbroke so craftily sought for himself has been his only to hold in trust. In the drama of history his role has been that of keeper of the crown, as Hal's has been that of the prince who must withdraw into seeming dishonor, playing truant to his royal calling, so that the stain of his father's usurpation will not discolor his own kingship in time to come.

We asked what debts Hal collects from Henry. Concerning true kingship Henry can hardly offer much. But then Hal does not demand much:

My gracious liege,
You won it, wore it, kept it, gave it to me.
Then plain and right must my possession be.
(lines 221–223)

The crown's the thing—not in itself, as seized possession, but as the symbol of regal inheritance. Possession of the crown may not guarantee true kingship—it certainly has not in Bolingbroke's case—but it is the *sine qua non* of the royal succession, the means by which an "honour snatched with boist'rous hand" can be transformed into "the garland [worn] successively," or what Hal calls "this lineal honour":

and put the world's whole strength
Into one giant arm, it shall not force

63

This lineal honour from me. This from thee
Will I to mine leave, as 'tis left to me.
(4.5.44–47)

The crown is the instrumental thing, but the succession is the thing itself, so powerful is Shakespeare's stress. The circular and tortured redundancy of Hal's last sentence—"This from thee / Will I to mine leave, as 'tis left to me"—helps hammer home the redemptive virtues of the royal succession, of lineal descent. Henry's death, as he says, "changes the mode." Because of him, history's scapegoat, Hal, can enter on kingship "in a more fairer sort" (4.5.201), relatively unburdened of guilt for the past, capable of creating "King Henry the Fifth" in his own image, after his own style, and yet conscious that "King" and "Henry" are two things and that the crown does not grow to his head. It is just this that was impossible in Richard's time, for the absolute fusion of "King" and "Richard" implied, at least in Richard's imagination, that the institution of kingship could not survive its incumbent. The price of Richard's autonomous Divine Rightness, pressed to such extremes of faith, was that it accompany him to the grave. Whoever followed Richard would of necessity "change the mode," for so long as his view of kingship prevailed there could be no such thing as a succession. "The King is dead; long live the King" could only be "Richard is dead; kingship is dead."

The "change of mode," then, liberates kingship from its corporeal bonds to Richard and makes possible a "line" of English kings. It also has a crucial bearing on the verbal issues discussed earlier. As I read him,

Shakespeare dramatizes his realization that the lie is the price language pays for metaphoric creativity. A fully monistic language of Richard's kind, a language of names invested with automatic truth and consonance to nature, though it looks appealing to the poet, would actually be a linguistic version of maximum entropy—a thought-benumbing collection of verbal signs pinned to a dead universe of things.[5] If in Richard's conception of kingship there can be no new kings (hence maximum political entropy), in a language directly bonded to nature there can be no new meanings. The price of infallible speech is a language and a nature mutually sealed off from change, as Edenic language and nature appear to have been before the beguiling satanic hiss introduced new and dangerous notions, among them newness itself.[6] Once divine authority and

5. Maximum entropy is of course a maximum extreme, not likely encountered. But the second law of linguistic thermodynamics holds good at more familiar ranges of experience too. When a culture still trusts its master metaphors after their semantic candlepower has dimmed, as the eighteenth century trusted the "great chain of being" metaphor and the twentieth century trusted Descartes' "ghost in the machine," or when living meanings surrender to cliché and platitude, or petrify into jargon, then the creative energies of symbolism have begun to dissipate, and the world turns gray.

6. In *De Vulgari Eloquentia* Dante spoke of Adam's language—Hebrew, he believed—as divinely created. It survived the confusion of tongues at Babel so that Christ "might use, not the language of confusion, but of grace" (I.vi). In canto 26 of the *Paradiso*, however, Dante speaks of language as created by reason and therefore subject to change:

human faith are withdrawn from such a language—once Richard is deposed—words must seem hopelessly disengaged from nature and quite incapable of transcending their fallen state. The emblems of this fallen state in politics are the counterfeit usurping king, in language the lie, and in drama that gross, open, palpable father of lies himself, Falstaff.

Despite the appeal of a monistic language, however, Shakespeare evidently perceives that automatic truth—truth where there is no possibility of error—is not truth at all but merely tautology, an endless reaffirmation of what is. If this is the case, then Shakespeare realizes also that his verbal art rests on the most unlikely of foundations, the lie. For without the possibility of the lie there can be neither creative metaphor, nor meaningful truth, nor in any authentic sense poetry. As with language, so with politics: without the possibility of counterfeit kings like Bolingbroke, there can be no genuine kings like Henry the Fifth. Not "genuine" in Richard's lost sense of having perfect title granted by God but genuine in the only ways kings can be in an imperfect world where no title is infallible but must be earned with the familiar human equipment —courage, sense of justice, intelligence, knowledge, all the old virtues that, from the nation's perspective, spring up so miraculously in the redeemed Hal.

----

                    for as they should,
    Like leaves upon the branches of a tree,
    The words of mortals die and are renewed.
    (lines 136–138; trans. Dorothy Sayers, New York, 1962)

The "renewing" is only possible in a language capable of change, as the poet in the act of creating meanings himself instinctively realizes.

Thus the poet can never be exempt from the charge of lying pressed by Platonic camp followers like Agrippa and Stephen Gosson. Nor, so long as he aspires to be a maker of meanings, should he want to be. Like the young Hal taking the dubious route through Eastcheap on his way to Westminster Abbey and his coronation, the poet must put his reputation in jeopardy, not only acknowledging the lie as part of the language he uses but even taking on its unprotective coloration, in order to claim his right to metaphor and his title to truth. From this perspective, to reinstitute royal succession in England is to restore to English itself nothing less than the verbal creativity without which poetry cannot survive.[7]

7. Sigurd Burckhardt ingeniously translated the Shakespearean stress on royal succession into a question of whether Shakespeare himself in the second tetralogy is to proceed with the lineal, successive development of his creative talents or to repeat his own earlier, orthodox treatment of history as a circular, repetitive, restorative process submissive to divine order, as he had done in the first tetralogy (*Shakespearean Meanings* [Princeton, 1968]). In Chapter 6 below I enlarge upon the present interpretation, joining the kingly succession to the Shakespearean dramatic succession in a way different from Burckhardt's. Before that can be done, however, there must be some sparring around with the endings of the two *Henry IV* plays.

・ 4 ・

1 *Henry IV:*

ART'S GILDED LIE

After the collapse of Richard II's divinely certified symbolism, Shakespeare begins *Henry IV* with a fallen language whose verbal emblem is the lie and whose human form is Falstaff, the corporealized lie. Falstaff, however, is by no means the only dealer in deception. As an interior playwright, Hal begins his drama of emergent royalty—which might be titled "The Prodigal Prince and the Reformed King"—with a lie, a deliberately beclouded identity by means of which he will "falsify men's hopes." Surrounded by counterfeit kings, he will counterfeit unkingliness himself so that in a belated recognition scene his suddenly revealed royalty will shine forth the more goodly to his English audience. Thus an unprincely lie will beget a most kingly truth. The effectiveness of Hal's strategy is suggested in the deathbed scene of 2 *Henry IV* when the lie (his "theft" of the crown, which makes him falsely appear both a callous son and a usurping prince) is made to yield the truth that he is both a loving son and a "true inheritor." Without the possibility of the lie there can be no truth, no new meanings, no creativity. Indeed, without the lie, drama is impossible.

The truth of this is particularly evident at the end of 1 *Henry IV* when Hal has just defeated Percy and thereby confirmed the validity of his claims to royalty. It is curious that precisely at this point, when he has proved himself a true prince among a field of counterfeit kings, Hal should again have recourse to the lie. For at this point he encounters a miraculously resurrected Falstaff carrying Percy on his final swaybacked ride, and Falstaff is quick to enter his own claim—if not to kingship, at least to knightly valor: "I grant you I was down and out of breath, and so was he. But we rose both at an instant and fought a long hour by Shrewsbury clock. If I may be believed, so . . ." (5.4. 149–152). Whether believed or not, Falstaff's lie calls forth another from Hal: "For my part, if a lie may do thee grace / I'll gild it with the happiest terms I have" (lines 161–162). To see what Hal's ornamenting lie entails let us go back a bit and observe Falstaff in the heat and heroism of battle.

In the middle of this scene (5.4) Hal and Hotspur, having exchanged precombat courtesies, begin their swordplay. Falstaff then enters and dances fiercely about the far fringes of the fray crying "Well said, Hal! To it, Hal! Nay, you shall find no boy's play here, I can tell you" (lines 75–76). It is a typical Falstaff remark, with the "you" being sufficiently vague to include the audience as well as the combatants. From our standpoint as audience, his denial raises what might otherwise have been an unconsidered possibility. For a disconcerting moment or two we may realize that "boy's play" is precisely what we shall find, are finding, here— mock combat, bated swords, the carefully rehearsed thrust and riposte, with Hotspur maneuvering surreptitiously to let Hal stab him in the vest pocket where a small bladder of pig's blood is concealed to make the groundlings grunt and the ladies squeal. Boy's play is as prominent here as it is a bit later when Douglas rushes on stage to pursue that great bladder of blood and sherris, the squealing Falstaff, who saws the air with his sword while hunting a comfortable place to collapse in mortal agony.

Still, as Hal and Hotspur fight expertly on, our imaginations are no doubt reabsorbed by the realities of fiction—by Hotspur's eloquent dying, surely, and Hal's graceful obsequy. If we have not seen the play before, we will continue to believe in the dramatic illusion as the bodies of Hotspur and Falstaff, equally dead to the best of our knowledge, lie side by side on stage. But if so, our belief is abruptly punctured when Falstaff pops up to announce that he has been only counterfeiting death:

> Counterfeit? I lie, I am no counterfeit.
> To die is to be a counterfeit, for he is but
> the counterfeit of a man who hath not the
> life of a man. But to counterfeit dying
> when a man thereby liveth is to be no
> counterfeit but the true and perfect image
> of life indeed.
>
> (lines 115–120)

Our uneasy suspicion that it is less the character Falstaff who speaks here than the actor who plays that character (since it is actors, not characters, who make a living by counterfeiting—by feigning to die, to love, to fight, to live at all) gains in conviction when Falstaff, glancing with mock nervousness at the "dead" body of Hotspur, says, " 'Zounds, I am afraid of this gunpowder Percy though he be dead. How if he should counterfeit too and rise? . . . Why may not he rise as well as I?" (lines 122–128). Why indeed? As Sigurd Burckhardt has said, "Not only *may* Hotspur rise but he will—as soon as the scene is ended and his 'body' has been lugged off the stage."[1]

Before Falstaff lugs off the body, however, he decides to make Percy "sure" by stabbing him again—"Yea, and I'll swear I killed him," he says (lines 126–127). It seems a safe enough plan, what with a dead Hotspur and a stage empty of witnesses. "Nothing confutes me but eyes," he says owlishly, "and nobody sees me" (lines 128–129). Again such a remark must give us pause. Given the sequence of metradramatic ironies already insinuated upon us—from "boy's play" to counterfeitings of life and death—Falstaff's statement here can hardly be kept tidily within the dramatic illusion of life. Like Falstaff himself, it bulges out of the realistic frame of fiction, calling attention to its own excess. Indeed, as he delivers the remark, Falstaff must peer about the empty stage, where nobody does observe him, and then turn and direct at his audience, at a whole theater of eyewitnesses, an enormous conspiratorial wink. And we in the audience—what are we to make of such a wink, and of all this puzzling Falstaffian doubletalk?

*

Burckhardt has argued that Falstaff rises from death as a symbol of disorder, a character who "out-

1. Sigurd Burckhardt, *Shakespearean Meanings* (Princeton, 1968), p. 147. Though my interpretation of Falstaff's rising, and of this scene in general, goes a different route from Burckhardt's, his are the seminal remarks and insights to which I am most indebted.

grew his preassigned measure and function" as foil to Hotspur. In refusing to remain conveniently dead he destroys dialectical symmetry—the notion that the conflict between Hotspur thesis and Falstaff antithesis yields the Prince Hal synthesis—and the symmetry between off-stage real life and on-stage illusions of life (or in this case illusions of death).[2] It seems to me that when Hal stands over the bodies of Hotspur and Falstaff the dialectical point is made whether Falstaff rises or not. But however it may be with dialectics, the symmetry Falstaff disturbs most significantly is not that obtaining between life and drama but that between drama in its two aspects, as mimesis of life (in this case, of English historical life) and as literary-theatrical artifice. In the former category we would refer to fiction, illusion, nature (what the illusion is *of*), realism, history; in the latter category, artificiality, theatricality, art, contrivance, entertainment.

It is probably true, as Burckhardt (and before him Brooks and Heilman)[3] suggested, that Falstaff outgrew his intended role and that in some degree he threatens the play itself just as, within the play, he threatens with comic laughter the high gravity of Henry's kingship and Hotspur's values. Thus in the present scene he has one foot inside the fiction of English history and the other outside it, turned to the audience—one foot planted in Shrewsbury soil and the other on the boards of the Theatre in Shoreditch. And why indeed shouldn't he? Hotspur accepts the reality of the fictional world of the play as wholeheartedly and (Falstaff would add)

2. Burckhardt, pp. 146–149.

3. Cleanth Brooks and Robert B. Heilman, *Understanding Drama* (New York, 1948), pp. 146–149.

as half-wittedly as he accepts, within that world, the pulsing reality of honor, truth, courage, glory. He can no more renounce his bond to fiction and confess that history is not history but theatrical illusion than he can interrupt his fight with Hal in midthrust and announce that this is not genuinely mortal combat but, as Falstaff slyly tells us, "boy's play." For history, after all, is Hotspur's proper domain. It is where, in Holinshed, Shakespeare discovered him; it is what he is designed to help recreate for the audience.

But Falstaff, whose origin is neither England's actual past nor Holinshed's pages, owes history nothing —not even if his name was once Oldcastle, "for Oldcastle died a martyr, and this is not the man" (2 *Henry IV*, Epilogue). Falstaff's origins are theatrical and literary: the Vice of morality tradition, the *miles gloriosus* and witty parasite of Plautine comedy, the clown-fool-butt-sponger-mocker-glutton of a thousand plays from Aristophanes to the anonymous author of *The Famous Victories of Henry the Fifth*. From Falstaff's theatrical perspective, Hotspur, Hal, Henry IV, Shrewsbury, and England herself are as insubstantial as Glendower's oft-called spirits from the vasty deep. Either divorced from the historical plot of usurpation and rebellion, or repudiating it with laughter, Falstaff is also divorced from the play as an illusion of historical life. His debts are not to the play as a mimesis of history but to the play as play—to the Shakespearean imagination that gave him life and to the audience for whose enjoyment he was given life.

At this point it would appear that Shakespeare conceives of these two dimensions of drama—mimesis and theatrics—as antagonistic, each devoted to its own brand of truth, its own species of reality or unreality. When Falstaff clambers up from death and declares that he lied in lying down, he is as he says the "true and perfect image of life indeed"—the life of the ever-living actor—and it is Percy, continuing to counterfeit death, who is the liar. But by refusing to stop counterfeiting, despite Falstaff's chiding, Percy remains true to *his* species of reality, to drama as simulated life. From this standpoint it is he who is the "true and perfect image of life"—the life of the character who imitates life, or death.

Normally, however, since this is essentially a realistic play unlike *Henry V*, Falstaff is obliged to operate in Percy's nontheatrical domain, where he becomes the father of lies and Percy the admired man of honor. Still, Falstaff does not operate wholly in this world—in it perhaps but not fully of it. If he cannot take the doings of kings and rebels seriously, neither can he take the whole realm of historical life, the mimetic dimension of the play, seriously. As a result he is endowed with the detachment essential to humor. From a mimetic standpoint he is a funny man, compounded of lies and japes. But he transcends and subverts mimetic reality. His costume is too flamboyant, his grease paint too obvious, his lies too transparent. Everyone he meets within the play he transforms immediately into an audience, most blatantly in 2.4 where he exhibits also his penchant for speaking over or through these interior audiences to Shakespeare's audience. Refusing to remain a character within and responsive to the world of historical life, he keeps asserting his "real" identity as a performer, imposing theatricality on history—hence his playing the fool and jester to Hal (or anyone), his comic lies designed not to persuade but to entertain (for example, the men in buckram and in Kendal green), his search for roles in which to display his histrionic genius, his constant readiness for drama ("What, shall we be merry? Shall we have a play extempore?" [2.4.307–308]).In these ways he momentarily extricates himself from the illusion of historical reality. But Shakespeare grants him the opportunity to break quite free from history and frolic in his native realm of theatrical artifice only once, when he lets him rise up from what for him (and us) would be a sorry death indeed: the cessation of stage life and a final thwarting of his need not merely to act (which is what the "dead" Hotspur is doing) but to act consciously, visibly, even ostentatiously.

*

In 5.4, with Falstaff clowning around in the realm of theater and taunting Hotspur for his stiff adherence to historical reality—with Falstaff proclaiming in effect that the emperor of mimetic drama has no clothes on—the two dimensions of *Henry IV* are in open antagonism, threatening to split the play irrevocably. Who knows?—an aroused Falstaff might walk right on out of the play and into the Admiral's Company, leaving behind a tawdry set of stage props and costumes, an embarrassed cast, and an audience plunged into bewilderment, an "alienation effect" of disastrous proportions. But Falstaff, as we have seen, confines his rebelliousness for the moment at least to a series of mocking double entendres. However, he is not yet finished. With Hotspur aloft he rocks over to the reentering Prince John and Hal and dumps his cargo. At

his unexpected reappearance Hal suffers something of
an alienation effect himself. "I saw him dead," he tells
John, "Breathless and bleeding on the ground. Art thou
alive? / Or is it fantasy that plays upon our eyesight?"
(lines 136–138).

Hal speaks here in character, so it seems, from
within the fiction. From our confused perspective, however, with Falstaff's exposures—in fact double exposures—before us, the line between mimesis and artifice, and between character and actor, may well
seem indistinct. Character may address character well
enough ("Art thou alive?") but we may also hear un-
dertones of actor addressing actor. What does Hal's
"fantasy" mean in this shifting context, or his "Thou
art not what thou seem'st" (line 140)? Is the actor Will
Kempe emerging from the character Falstaff? Something entirely different rather: Falstaff may expand to
include Will Kempe. Falstaff is a character whose role
is to play the actor. If Kempe may play Falstaff, may
not Falstaff play Kempe? Not the historical Kempe, of
course, but Kempe as the generic actor.

However we register the ambiguities, Hal attempts
to remain—with Percy dumped "dead" at his feet—
inside the historical fiction. The result, from Falstaff's
liberated perspective, is that Hal lies twice in one sentence, when he says, "Why, Percy I killed myself and
saw thee dead" (line 147). "Didst thou?" Falstaff cries,
miming appeals to heaven:

> Didst thou? Lord, Lord, how this world is given
> to lying! I grant you I was down and out of breath,
> and so was he. But we rose both at an instant and
> fought a long hour by Shrewsbury clock. If I may
> be believed, so; if not, let them that should reward

valour bear the sin upon their own heads. I'll take it upon my death, I gave him this wound in the thigh.

(lines 148–155)

The double exposure of character and actor, of realistic life and theatrical art, remains in ambiguous force in this speech. In terms of dramatic "life" the character Falstaff is typically capitalizing on circumstance, improvising his way toward his only notion of nobility: "I look to be either earl or duke, I can assure you" (lines 145–146). From the standpoint of dramatic "art" Falstaff, the character whose role is that of the actor, is threatening Hal and the play with exposure: "You know and I know that you didn't kill Hotspur any more than Douglas killed me. Of course I didn't kill him either, but I can claim as much as you, and lie a lot better. If Percy here weren't so deafened by his honor he'd stand up and prove us both liars. But he won't. So, my sweet young prince, we are at a stand-off. Expose me as a liar and I'll expose you in return. And where's your fine play then?"

Percy, Falstaff has already exposed as a liar, but Percy, true to history, could not get up and deny it; he *did* die at Shrewsbury. Hal, however, has more latitude, which is to say a more flexible consciousness and a less radical devotion to honor. Though he belongs to the world of history, he has never achieved, nor quite attempted, Hotspur's leap of faith into the play as mimesis of life. If Falstaff has been entertaining audiences inside and outside the play, Hal has lent his assistance willingly. It is he who directs the "exposure" of Falstaff in the Boar's Head Tavern after Gadshill,

77

setting the stage, supplying Falstaff with leading questions, acting as straight man. "What trick, what device, what starting-hole canst thou now find out to hide thee from this open and apparent shame?" (2.4.289–292)—what more friendly leg up to a devastating reply could Falstaff desire? If Falstaff is delighted to exhibit his verbal dexterity at this point, Hal is no less delighted to exhibit Falstaff, like an animal trainer with a trick bear. And a little later in the scene Hal proves as ready to turn histrionic and play royal as Falstaff, though with his concluding "I do, I will" he is disposed to convert the play-acting from idle entertainment into a rehearsal of future history. That is appropriate too, because as a future king Hal knows very well that his business is to shape history, not to be shaped by it. To Hotspur history is a fixed and final reality to which he is irrevocably committed. He has given his word, as it were: he cannot alter his role. To Hal on the other hand history is a series of roles and staged events. He creates for himself the role of princely roisterer as a means of dramatizing to good advantage his conversion to the regal role of Henry the Fifth. Both as actor-dramatist of his own royal play, then, and as part-time sharer in Falstaff's theatrics, Hal knows perfectly well that the emperor of mimetic drama is without clothes.

*

The aesthetic fact which this scene revolves around is that all plays aspiring to the illusion of life are vulnerably naked unless their audiences clothe them from the wardrobe of imagination. Shakespeare's audience probably suspended disbelief as willingly as any other, transforming Will Kempe with a pillow stuffed beneath his doublet into Falstaff, a stage full of costumed actors playing soldier into the battle of Shrewsbury Field, and Shakespearean blank verse into the speech of living and dying men. So of course do we—a generation of playgoers raised on Pirandello, Brecht, Anouilh, Beckett, Pinter, and Genet—for the play will not work otherwise. We cannot be simultaneously conscious of actor and character, of theater and depicted life, of art and nature. We cannot be imaginatively involved in the immediate experience of the play and, at the same time, be intellectually detached from it, playgoer and critic at once, any more than we can register Hamlet's feeling while deliberating on Gielgud's competence in the role, or take in the meaning of a soliloquy while parsing the lines.[4] Yet that is the unhappy plight into which Falstaff's withdrawal from the fiction of history thrusts us. With the illusion of heroic life shattered, we are left confronting the trumpery of theater—costumes, actors, props, stage, words issuing from a script instead of from men's mouths. Lord, Lord, how this theater is given to lying! So the truth-loving Falstaff tells us—to be echoed in latter days by Pirandello, Brecht, Ionesco, and many others. Perhaps Hal too would join in admitting art's shortcomings; but less distrustful of the imagination and the illusions it helps foster than a Brecht or an Ionesco, Hal accepts the practical necessity of the lie. For if the play is not to split down the middle, Falstaff must be made

4. Northrop Frye has some pertinent remarks on the discreteness of literary criticism and the direct experience of literature in *Anatomy of Criticism* (Princeton, 1957), pp. 27–28.

to abandon his theatrical indulgences and reenter the world of fiction.

So Hal abandons his claim to having killed Percy in return for Falstaff's abandoning his claim to purely theatrical life: "Come, bring your luggage nobly on your back. / For my part, if a lie may do thee grace, / I'll gild it with the happiest terms I have" (5.4.160–162). The bond is sealed as Falstaff hoists (and so acknowledges the "deadness" of?) the dead Percy onto his back and complacently accepts an ironic parting shot from Hal, who says to Prince John, "Come, brother, let us to the highest of the field, / To see what friends are living, who are dead" (lines 164–165). Falstaff's final lines in the scene, and in the play, express his willingness to reform if the price is right: "I'll follow as they say, for reward. He that rewards me, God reward him! If I do grow great, I'll grow less; for I'll purge and leave sack and live cleanly as a nobleman should do" (lines 166–169). The price Hal has already paid is one that Percy would never suffer, a lie; but what is bought with Hal's lie is a restoration of the mode of dramatic reality to which Percy was so totally committed. Historical truth may be violated (though Holinshed does not say who killed Percy at Shrewsbury, it was certainly not Falstaff), but the mimesis of historical life is preserved. If theatrical illusion is a lie, it is a lie that must be countenanced, for there can be no theater without it.

It is highly fitting that Hal should mediate at this point between the claims of Hotspur mimesis and Falstaff theatrics because he has, as I've suggested, had a foot in each or a hand in both already—he whose origin is history but whose self-contrived drama of kingship relies on his playing off the character of the wastrel Hal against that of the reformed Henry V. In each dimension of the play Hal has served to unite or at least to mediate between Falstaff and Hotspur. Thus in Percy's world—in the play as realistic mimesis of historical life—the character Hal may be regarded as possessing the best features of the two mighty opposites. Or, so the variations have run, he may be seen as an Aristotelian golden mean between their excesses and defects, a Christian-Platonic ideal liberated from their imperfections, a happy commingling of the "humours" that flow singly or sluggishly in the others, a synthesis that transcends dialectical contraries, and so on.[5] Whichever we choose, Hal is seen as standing somehow between or over Hotspur and Falstaff, as he literally does over their apparently dead bodies at Shrewsbury. Similarly in Falstaff's world—in the play as unrealistic work of theatrical art—it is Hal's victories at Gadshill and Shrewsbury, his capacity to move with ease between the Percy sphere of high history and the Falstaff sphere of high jinks, between the blank verse of the one and the colorful prose of the other, that stitch together the two plots of the

5. See for example: William B. Hunter, "Prince Hal, His Struggle for Moral Perfection," *South Atlantic Quarterly* 50 (1951): 86–95, for the Aristotelian mean; J. Dover Wilson, *The Fortunes of Falstaff* (New York, 1944), for a morality play view with Christian-Platonic overtones; U. C. Knoepflmacher, "The Humors as Symbolic Nucleus in *Henry IV*, Part I," *College English* 24 (1963): 497–501, for the commingling of humors in Hal; and Hiram Haydn, *The Counter-Renaissance* (New York, 1950), pp. 598–605, for an Aristotelian and Platonic view of Hal in terms of the concept of honor.

play and thus impart to *Henry IV* an aesthetic, structural coherence to which drama as a mimesis of life is indifferent. Finally, since Hal's ultimate function in history is to reunite an England torn throughout his father's reign by dissension, it is appropriate that his dramaturgical function at this point be to reunite a play that is itself splitting into antagonistic factions.

Before leaving the issue of Hal's fitness to mediate between Hotspur and Falstaff, let me glance at one more famous piece of evidence—the moment when he stands over the two bodies and takes verbal leave of each (5.4.87–110).

> Fare thee well, great heart!
> Ill-weaved ambition, how much art thou shrunk!
> When that this body did contain a spirit,
> A kingdom for it was too small a bound.
> But now two paces of the vilest earth
> Is room enough. This earth that bears thee dead
> Bears not alive so stout a gentleman.
> If thou wert sensible of courtesy
> I should not make so dear a show of zeal.
> But let my favours hide thy mangled face,
> And, even in thy behalf, I'll thank myself
> For doing these fair rites of tenderness.
> Adieu, and take thy praise with thee to heaven!
> Thy ignominy sleep with thee in the grave,
> But not remembered in thy epitaph.
> [*He spieth Falstaff on the ground.*]
> What, old acquaintance, could not all this flesh
> Keep in a little life? Poor Jack, farewell!
> I could have better spared a better man.
> O, I should have a heavy miss of thee
> If I were much in love with vanity!
> Death hath not struck so fat a deer today,

Art's Gilded Lie

Though many dearer in this bloody fray.
Embowelled will I see thee by and by;
Till then in blood by noble Percy lie.

[*Exit.*]

Here we have the crowning visual symbol—Hal standing over the two—of a relationship that has existed
throughout the play, and it is a commonplace to observe
that Hal's remarks characterize Hotspur as all spirit
(lines 89–90) and Falstaff as all flesh (lines 102–103),
each limited and partial while Hal combines both in
the full human reality. What I would prefer to em-
phasize here is how the obsequies are stylistically
geared not merely to the different natures of the two
men but also to the different modes of dramatic reality in which they live, and now "die." In brief, Hal
plays it straight with Hotspur, giving him a graceful
send-off in keeping with the moving eloquence of Hotspur's dying words. Hotspur *is* dead; the style of
Hal's obsequy confirms it—and we are safer trusting
style than apparent facts in drama. Because Hal assumes Hotspur's mode of reality here, which means
accepting his death, he can say "If thou wert sensible
of courtesy / I should not make so dear a show of zeal"
(5.4.93–94). To be sure. But there on the other side of
Hal lies a "dead" Falstaff, ears flared wide, who *is*
"sensible of courtesy" (and discourtesy), a Falstaff who
is gathering himself for a comic resurrection as soon as
Hal turns his back. How, then, does Hal address him?
Precisely as if he knew he were faking death. He delivers a brief speech full of ironic puns that hold out
a "courtesy" with one hand and discourteously jerk it
back again with the other: "better spared a better

83

man . . . heavy miss of thee . . . so fat a deer . . . Though many dearer." He also introduces a closing phrase—"Embowelled will I see thee by and by"—that drops a verbal ladder into Falstaff's grave and invites him back into comic life: "Embowelled! If thou embowel me today, I'll give you leave to powder and eat me too tomorrow!" (lines 111–113). And Hal ends with a pun on a crucial word: "Till then in blood by noble Percy *lie*" (line 110). This, when in a moment we will discover that the prostrate Falstaff has been "lying" in both senses all the while!

How to interpret this? Only in a very curious sense, I suppose, could we say that the character Hal "knows" that Falstaff is not dead and so speaks to him on his own theatrical level, while on the other hand, knowing that Percy is not "really" dead either, he nevertheless accepts the Percy mode of illusion and addresses him realistically. I think we are justified in making somewhat similar claims about Falstaff and Hal later in this scene because the theatrical ironies from Falstaff's "counterfeiting" speech onward are too sustained, obvious, and logically consistent to ignore. But Hal's "If thou wert sensible of courtesy" is embedded in a realistic context and functions adequately there; and one could say the same of his punning speech over Falstaff—that its light chiding style suits the occasion because it suits the nature of their friendship and that by means of humorous understatement it suggests in Hal a depth of feeling that would have looked specious otherwise. Perhaps the most we would want to claim, then, is that Hal's speech reflects Shakespeare's desire not to make him look foolish, that the style and tone of the speech are conditioned not by

Hal's but by Shakespeare's knowledge that the "dead" Falstaff remains fully "sensible of courtesy." That seems about right, unless we are troubled by the fact that every character's speeches are conditioned by the omniscience of the playwright. So whether we impute to Hal an awareness beyond that possible to a realistic character or not, the dramatic fact is that his lines to Hotspur and Falstaff register the differences between the two modes of death, the realistic and the theatrical, and mark Hal as the one character who can come to terms with both. He responds to Hotspur's death seriously and to Falstaff's lightly, precisely as he can make sport of Falstaff at Gadshill and kill Percy at Shrewsbury. This flexibility enables him not only to unite a divided England but to unite a temporarily divided *Henry IV* as well.

*

When Falstaff is lured back into the historical fiction it may appear that theatrical drama is sacrificed to mimetic drama. It is true that Falstaff surrenders his right, or license, to stand outside the fiction and mock its claims to truth. But what, after all, is Falstaff without the fictional life within the play? His domain is hardly that of real life; he cannot walk out of the Boar's Head Tavern and into the Mermaid Tavern in Bread Street. And so long as he is confined to the stage he cannot, however well-stocked with suety sustenance, survive for long without a play to feed on. Unless he hopes to initiate vaudeville,[6] he and the hu-

6. After writing this I ran across some perceptive remarks about the theatricality of Falstaff by Arthur Sewell in *Character and Society in Shakespeare* (Oxford, 1951):

mor he energizes must replenish themselves from the sideboards of historical life. This is surely part of the "reward" he will find within the play as he follows Hal and Prince John back to Shrewsbury and on to 2 *Henry IV*.

If Falstaff relinquishes the autonomous truth of theatrical art by reentering the fiction, Hal relinquishes the autonomous truth of historical life by supporting Falstaff's lie with one of his own. Neither dimension of drama, it is apparent, can exist without the other, though for a moment, caught in Falstaff's double exposure image, they seemed disastrously separable. If theater, for much of this scene, has obscured our view

---

"Falstaff is aware of his audience, on and off the stage, and the comic artistry is part of the comic character. His life within the play—the only life he has—is a sustained vaudeville turn. The audience is necessary to his being" (p. 34). The notion of vaudeville is good insofar as it distinguishes Falstaff from the other characters, those fully devoted to the play as realistic illusion of life, but it is not so good if it suggests that his humor is somehow independent from this dimension of the play. In 2 *Henry IV* Falstaff says, "I am not only witty in myself but the cause that wit is in other men" (1.2.11–12). But the reverse is quite as true, that his wittiness and especially his burlesque humor are made possible by the other characters who are playing their roles straight—Hotspur, Henry IV, Hal at times, Mistress Quickly, the Lord Chief Justice, Justice Shallow, and others.

Eugene P. Nassar has some excellent remarks about the way in which Shakespearean characters can slip out of their realistic roles in what Nassar calls the "core drama" and deliver lines conditioned by Shakespeare's artistic or theatrical intentions—see "Shakespeare's Games with His Audience" in Nassar's *The Rape of Cinderella* (Bloomington, Ind., and London, 1970), pp. 100–19.

of dramatic life, it now dissolves into transparency again, seemingly disappearing but remaining in fact as a lens through which we witness the mimesis of history. By a process of mutual sacrifice, art and nature are realigned and the life of the play restored.

But the price, we must remember, is a lie. Or, to put a kinder construction on it, perhaps we should say that the price is a liberalizing of the imagination, a setting aside of the standards of fact and reason that give rise to the notions of true and false in real life. From this standpoint the lie is the test of our poetic faith, our ticket to literature. Once inside the literary domain, we may discover that the lie has proven a road to truths otherwise denied the truth-loving mind. But for the moment we may feel that readmitting Falstaff to the play, especially on his own blackmailing terms, carries ominous suggestions for 2 *Henry IV*, toward which we may glance with one auspicious and one dropping eye.

5

2 *Henry IV:*

THE EMBODIED NAME
AND THE REJECTED MASK

In the last chapter I suggested that Falstaff rises up from pseudo-death to create a disconcerting double exposure of art and nature. As a rebel against realism he threatens a secession of the theatrical from the mimetic aspects of the play. Such a cleavage would leave *Henry IV* as split into warring factions as the characters within it. At Shrewsbury, however, Hal proves himself the queller of rebellions, the reunifier—a military and political role that is analogous to his dramaturgical role as the main unifier of Shakespeare's play. In the monetary imagery so prominent in *Henry IV*, Hal at Shrewsbury figures once again as the man who pays off, the redeemer who has just saved his father's life and crown, "paid" Percy, and rescued his own sorry reputation. His final act is to quell Falstaff's "rebellion," not with a sword—Falstaff has already refused to submit to death on stage—but with verbal coin. The price of Falstaff's return to fiction is his lie, "gilded" with the happiest terms Hal can summon (5.4.161–162). This verbal glitter, insofar as Falstaff accepts it as down-payment on a debt he expects to be paid gloriously in full when Hal is crowned, turns out to be fool's gold when assayed at Westminster Abbey. In the meantime, however, Falstaff follows Hal back into the play, "for reward" (5.4.166), and dramatic unity is purchased by the acceptance of counterfeit coin.

Falstaff's lie at Shrewsbury is sustained in 2 *Henry IV*, fittingly lodged in that lie-ridden, rumor-governed play in which Shakespeare spins out the consequences of the fall of sacramental speech. I have already treated that issue in purely linguistic terms (see chapter 2). In the present chapter I want to consider how Hal's acceptance and gilding of Falstaff's lie in 1 *Henry IV*, 5.4, influences the characterization of Falstaff in 2 *Henry IV* and how this in turn bears ultimately on the rejection scene at Westminster.

However misleading it may be, the lie Hal gilds at Shrewsbury is creative. It invests Falstaff with an identity, gives him a "name" in the historical world, a place in the story.[1] Much earlier, when Hal was arming himself psychologically for Shrewsbury, he assured his dubious father that Percy was merely his "factor," a collector of honors, titles, and glorious deeds, all of which would be delivered over to Hal when they met in combat (1 *Hen. IV*, 3.3.129–159). At Shrewsbury, however, Hal no sooner collects from Percy than he is obliged in his turn to play factor to Falstaff, his name-gatherer. This is appropriate enough since Falstaff has for some time been in search of names. "I would to God," he lamented to Hal earlier, "thou and I knew

1. See chapter 3 for an interpretation of the Shrewsbury encounter between Hal and Hotspur as a contest for name and title. These, collected from Hotspur by Hal, are then transferred into the dubious safekeeping of Falstaff.

where a commodity of good names were to be bought"
(1 *Henry IV*, 1.2.92–94). While Hal has spent his time
learning the speech and names of his future subjects—
so well that he "can call them all their christen names
as Tom, Dick, and Francis"—Falstaff has sought
through friendship with the future king (gilt by association) to acquire a name of his own, not for the sake
of the name itself—he is no Percy or latterday Richard
II—but for its purchasing powers. At Shrewsbury,
then, he buys up a commodity of good names from
Percy through his broker Hal, and throughout 2 *Henry
IV* he lives off the credit of his new reputation. Even
the Chief Justice admits ruefully, "Your day's service
at Shrewsbury hath a little gilded [!] over your night's
exploit on Gadshill" (1.2.168–169). So richly has it
gilded it over that Falstaff is employed as the king's
recruiter in warrior-rich Gloucestershire, where his
noble reputation serves him well. Later, after the rebel
leaders have surrendered to Prince John at Gaultree, it
is Falstaff's lie-gotten name as a knight of prowess and
honor that persuades Colville of the Dale to surrender
to him: "I think you are Sir John Falstaff, and in that
thought yield me" (4.3.18–19). Colville's astonishing
surrender fulfills Falstaff's prophetic complaint to the
Chief Justice in the opening act: "I would to God my
name were not so terrible to the enemy as it is"
(1.2.144–146).

Falstaff's name had grown somewhat terrible to
his allies even before it brought his enemies quailing
before him. Mistress Quickly, whose sexual surrenders
probably do not need the prompting of a fierce reputation, has in more important matters apparently been
so persuaded by Falstaff's new claims to honor and

substance that she has allowed him once again to become "an infinitive thing upon [her] score" (2.1.26).
Rebuked by the Chief Justice for his failure to repay
his debts to her, Falstaff replies in the manner of one
well-puffed with the insolence of official station:

> You call honorable boldness impudent sauciness;
> if a man will make curtsy and say nothing, he is
> virtuous. No, my lord, my humble duty remem-
> bered, I will not be your suitor. I say to you, I do
> desire deliverance from these officers, being upon
> hasty employment in the King's affairs.
>
> (2.1.134–140)

To which the Chief Justice replies indignantly, "You
speak as having power to do wrong." The name is more
and more becoming the man. The man, at any rate,
has increasing recourse to the name. When he opens
his letter to Prince Hal with the words "John Falstaff,
knight," Poins, reading it to Hal, drily observes that
"every man must know that, as oft as he has occasion
to name himself—even like those that are kin to the
King, for they never prick their finger but they say
'There's some of the King's blood spilt'" (2.2.118–
124). The justice of Poins's observation is confirmed by
the close of Falstaff's letter:

> Thine, by yea and no, which is as much as to say,
> as thou usest him, JACK FALSTAFF with my familiars,
> JOHN with my brothers and sisters, and SIR JOHN
> with all Europe.
>
> (2.2.142–146)

This pomposity rivals Pistol's, and surely Doll Tear-
sheet's tirade on Pistol's use of the title "Captain" must
ricochet in Falstaff's direction too:

Captain! Thou abominable damned cheater, art
thou not ashamed to be called captain? An captains
were of my mind, they would truncheon you out
for taking their names upon you before you have
earned them. You a captain! You slave, for what?
For tearing a poor whore's ruff in a bawdy-house?

(2.4.151–157)

If Falstaff's name was not earned *by* him, it certainly earns *for* him—with Mistress Quickly in London of course, but also in Gloucestershire where, having the power to do wrong, Falstaff does it, cashing in
on his title and official function by accepting bribes
from prospective soldiers and by setting up Justice
Shallow for a thousand-pound loan. The value of his
name is demonstrated most obviously, however, when
Colville of the Dale surrenders to him at Gaultree.
Though Falstaff says of Colville to Prince John, "He
saw me and yielded" (4.3.43–44), in fact Colville surrendered not to Falstaff but to his name. If there is a
sense in which the fat knight himself is being subordi-
nated to or absorbed by his name there is another sense
in which his name is being absorbed by and into him:
"I have," he replies to Colville's request of his name,
"a whole school of tongues in this belly of mine, and
not a tongue of them all speaks any other word but my
name" (4.3.20–22). In his belly full of tongues pronouncing "Sir John" (presumably to "all Europe"), we
have the total corporealization of the Falstaffian name.
The caloric Word has become, if not flesh, lard.

With Falstaff depicted for us as a great name-
singing belly we can more easily perceive the significance of Warwick's speech of reassurance to King
Henry:

The Prince but studies his companions
Like a strange tongue, wherein to gain the language
'Tis needful that the most immodest word
Be looked upon and learned—which once attained,
Your Highness knows, comes to no further use
But to be known and hated. So, like gross terms,
The Prince will in the perfectness of time
Cast off his followers. And their memory
Shall as a pattern or a measure live
By which his Grace must mete the lives of others.
Turning past evils to advantages.

(2 *Hen. IV*, 4.4.67–78)

The prince must reject Falstaff no doubt for many reasons. One of them is implied in the argument we have been tracing, the climax of which is the metaphoric union of name and body in Falstaff. Falstaff is no longer separable from his name—from the identity he has assumed within the historical fiction. In this regard he has undergone a radical change from the Falstaff of Part 1.

In Part 1, as discussed earlier, Falstaff is largely a theatrical creation possessed of a histrionic self-consciousness that makes him seem not fully "of" the play, as Percy on the other hand so completely is. He is less an actor playing the role of a character than a character playing the role of an actor. He "acts" and "lies" throughout the play not merely to extricate himself from threatening situations (he is quite invulnerable to threats because the realistic dimension of the play is from his theatrical standpoint "unreal") but because these are, as it were, his profession, and it is no sin for a man to labor in his profession. That is, he acts and lies not to deceive audiences (either those within the play, such as Hal and Poins, or those out-side the play, in the theater) into believing what he says and does—that is Hotspur's realistic strategy—but to gratify his own talents and to make us enjoy his acting as acting, his lying as lying.

Falstaff's last act of Part 1, however, is to sur-render his theatricality, and his claim to being a true man, in return for Hal's granting him a name and an identity in the historical fiction. Whereas he was essen-tially invulnerable in Part 1 because his "true" life was not rooted in the illusion of historical reality, now he has become most vulnerable indeed. Early in Part 2 he tells us that he is afflicted with consumption of the purse, with gout, fatness, and age (1.1.264–278). These are of course old ailments, but in Part 1 they had only a kind of instrumental stage reality as comic devices to be levied on for humor. Now they belong to the man, who no longer merely uses them but feels them. In 2.4, for instance, when Doll wonders when Falstaff will "begin to patch up [his] old body for heaven," he replies without humor:

> Peace, good Doll! Do not speak like a death's
> head. Do not bid me remember mine end.
> (2.4.252–255)

There follows a series of exchanges in which Falstaff is induced to ridicule Hal and Poins, who are standing behind him disguised as drawers; and then Falstaff suddenly interjects the remark "I am old, I am old" (2.4.294), as though during the intervening comic ex-changes his mind has never really left that sobering thought.

The effect of this change in Falstaff is that, while

he remains full of lies and japes, he appears to us as a realistic character—humorous still but with an underlying desolateness also (I don't mean to give him a tragic turn, but there is a forecast of his quasi-pathetic death in *Henry V*)—who must rouse himself to meet occasions, who must almost wearily at times put on the blown, puffy style and the comic mask. His acting and lying are no longer the brilliant tools of the comic escape artist but the instruments of a very felt human need. In Part 1 Falstaff was the constant victim—of Hal, Poins, Douglas, his own weight and bulk. The most frequent comic technique of the play was to put him in a tight spot and then watch his footwork. But in Part 2 Falstaff, victimized by his own needs, makes victims of others—Mistress Quickly, the Gloucestershire conscripts, Justice Shallow, Colville of the Dale, and in the offing, he hopes, Henry the Fifth. He acts, lies, plays the role of Sir John to all Europe, not as pleasurable and entertaining activities in themselves, but as tactics of exploitation. He addresses himself more and more *to* his fellow characters rather than, as in Part 1, both to them and over them to the audience. His acting, in short, is increasingly genuine, springing from his material needs as a character within the fiction.[2]

2. Naturally there are exceptions to this. The realism of his acting is qualified, for instance, by the fact that he delivers several asides to the audience, as C. L. Barber observes in *Shakespeare's Festive Comedy* (Princeton, 1959), p. 215. These asides occur at the end of 1.2 ("I will turn diseases to commodity"), at the end of 3.2 when he comments on Shallow's reminiscences ("Lord, Lord, how subject we old men are to this vice of lying"), and at the end of 4.3 in his speech on sherris-sack after his capture of

In this sense, I suggest, Falstaff has "become" his new identity, has swallowed up his fictional role, and thus become the embodiment, or embellyment, of his name. The seriousness with which he takes himself now is never more evident than on his learning of the death of Henry IV:

> I know the young king is sick for me Let us take any man's horses; the laws of England are at my commandment. Blessed are they that have been my friends, and woe to my Lord Chief Justice!
>
> (5.4.141–145)

Or, again, when he stands along the coronation route contemplating the effect on Hal of his dishevelment: "this doth infer the zeal I had to see him."

> *Shallow*: It doth so.
>   *Fals*: It shows my earnestness of affection—
> *Shallow*: It doth so.
>   *Fals*: My devotion.
> *Shallow*: It doth, it doth, it doth!
>   *Fals*: As it were, to ride day and night, and not to deliberate, not to remember, not to have patience to shift me. . . .
>
> (5.5.15–23)

In the calculus of greed and need Falstaff's rhetoric is wonderfully persuasive not merely to the violently

---

Colville. In their form, as asides, these speeches should call attention to the unreality, the theatricality, of Falstaff, but in their content the reverse is true. That is, because in each instance Falstaff dilates upon his material needs—created by diseases, consumption of the purse, old age, and bodily appetite—the asides do not suggest his artificiality but, somewhat like Hamlet's soliloquies, deepen and confirm our sense of his fictional reality.

nodding Justice Shallow but to Falstaff himself, who once knew better.

*

In "becoming" his new identity Falstaff accepts Hotspur's dimension of dramatic reality and so acquires something of Hotspur's inflexibility as a character, his inability to be other than what he is, a presumably "real" person making his way in a "real" world. Even within this world Falstaff has some light resemblances to Hotspur. Oblivious to the forecasts of rejection Hal has given out, to the gravity of the state occasion at Westminster, and to the impact of kingship on Hal, Falstaff seems afflicted with Hotspur's "situation deafness"—his incapacity to register the nuances of tone and meaning that distinguish situations and call for appropriately varied responses. Surely we are meant to see in Falstaff, the horsed knight hotly spurring toward Westminster, some comic likeness to Hotspur charging pell-mell into battle and a grave at Shrewsbury—each of them plunging myopically toward his separate doom dreaming on glories to come. Falstaff's gushing "My king! My Jove! I speak to thee, my heart!" (5.5.50) is in its own fashion as witlessly suicidal as Hotspur's "Doomsday is near— die all, die merrily!" (2 *Hen. IV*, 4.1.134). This parallel would imply of course that Hal kills Falstaff at Westminster as he did Percy at Shrewsbury.

Another comparison to be mentioned is that between Falstaff and Pistol, who in some respects stands at the opposite pole from Percy yet resembles him too. Whereas Hotspur lives unalterably in the "real" world of history, at the furthest remove from the poetic and literary (with which Glendower is associated in 1 *Henry IV*), Pistol seems to have stumbled by accident into *Henry IV*, having fallen from the awesome heights of a Marlovian tragedy or perhaps a Spanish tragedy written by Don Armado of *Love's Labour's Lost*.[3] Perfectly identified with and inseparable from his role as tragic fantastico, Pistol imposes his King Cambyses style and conception of reality on everyone he meets, usually to their wide-eyed bewilderment.

Nevertheless it is no accident that Falstaff rides to Westminster *with* Pistol and in some degree *like* Hotspur. For though Pistol and Hotspur come from different realms of being, they have something in common. Both are unselfconscious in their acting, are welded to their roles, and take themselves with surpassing seriousness. If Hotspur suffers from situation-deafness, Pistol is situation-deafness itself. All occasions, however various, are filtered through the close mesh of his fancy and transformed into the stuff of bombastic melodrama: "A foutra for the world and worldlings base! I speak of Africa and golden joys" (5.3.103–104). Hotspur too, though rooted in history and realism, can rise to Pistollian O altitudos himself—most notably during his expostulations about "Mortimer" and honor after Henry IV demanded the return of his prisoners (1 *Henry IV*, 1.3.125–258).

It is the superheated spur and the exploding pistol, then—characters quite carried away from reality by racing bloodstreams or fanatical fancies—that Falstaff resembles as he rushes to Westminster. Rejected by Hal, Falstaff returns to the cold hillside of reality ab-

3. See in this connection Anne Righter's fine book *Shakespeare and the Idea of the Play* (London, 1962), pp. 140–143.

ruptly—"Master Shallow, I owe you a thousand pound" (5.5.77–78). A sudden descent from "Sir John with all Europe." But not even the cudgel-enforced eating of Fluellen's leek can reveal a genuine man behind the bizarre tragic mask of Pistol; he sticks to his role—"All hell shall stir for this!" (*Hen. V*, 5.1.72). In Pistol's final lines in *Henry V* (5.1.85–94), however, we *do* see the face behind the mask. But it is not Pistol's face, it is Falstaff's![4]

To return, however, to present concerns. At Westminster Falstaff has taken up a stance at the opposite extreme from his Shrewsbury ward. At Shrewsbury he stepped outside the mimesis of historical life and from the standpoint of art's contrivances launched a mocking attack on the "reality" of the play's realism. In 2 *Henry IV*, however, he has accepted that reality, has (in both senses) invested himself in his fictional identity, and now threatens the play from within. The threat is two-pronged. It aims on the one hand at the play's historical truth and on the other at its dramatic decorum.

In the first connection we should observe that although Falstaff has hitherto entered into the historical fiction of *Henry IV* he has not by and large entered into history. Roistering in the Boar's Head Tavern, jibing at the Lord Chief Justice in the streets, exploiting the natives in Gloucestershire, even capturing Colville of the Dale (who is merely a name in Holinshed)—

---

4. The lines at the end of *Henry V*, 5.1—beginning "Doth Fortune play the huswife with me now?" (lines 85–94)— are spoken by Pistol but appear to have been written originally for Falstaff and then left unaltered after Falstaff was removed from the play.

these are one thing. But riding any man's horses not merely to the coronation but beyond it and into the actual reign of Henry the Fifth, that is another thing. Falstaff can no more enter history itself, without a gross violation of history, than Hotspur could forswear history and rise up from his "death" at Shrewsbury. Yet that is what Falstaff proposes to do, threatening forcible entry at one of English history's most august and ceremonially fortified gates: "God save thy Grace, King Hal, my royal Hal!" (5.5.45). Thus he must be turned away.

If truth to history requires that Falstaff be turned away, the decorum of a history *play* requires that he be in effect done away with. To read "death" into Hal's chilly rejection, in other words, we need not seek corroboration outside drama, in purgation rituals and notions of Oedipal patricide, as some critics have (illuminatingly) done.[5] Entirely in literary or dramatic terms Hal may be said to kill Falstaff at Westminster, though the dying lingers on into *Henry V* where it takes place quietly offstage, perhaps for fear Falstaff would leap up again roaring "Play out the play; I have much to say in behalf of that Falstaff!" In any event Hal's murder weapons at Westminster are style and decorum. Stylistically Falstaff is quite thrust through by the

5. See Ernst Kris, "Prince Hal's Conflict" in his *Psychoanalytic Explorations in Art* (New York, 1952), pp. 273–288; J. I. M. Stewart's "The Birth and Death of Falstaff" in his *Character and Motive in Shakespeare* (London, 1949), pp. 111–139; C. L. Barber's "Rule and Misrule in *Henry IV*" in his *Shakespeare's Festive Comedy* (Princeton, 1959), pp. 192–221; and Philip Williams's "The Birth and Death of Falstaff Reconsidered," *Shakespeare Quarterly* 8 (1957): 359–365.

entire rejection speech, in which Hal for the first time addresses him in blank verse. Such verse has a cutting edge at this point because, as opposed to the nonhistorical world's racy prose, it is the distinctive style of history—most notably of Hotspur, who almost never descends to prose, but also of Henry IV and the other nobles and even of Hal when in historical company.[6] Thus Hal implicitly demands from Falstaff a verse style that he, comic master of verbal variety though he is, can by no means sustain beyond a few quick passes of parody. From this perspective, if Falstaff *could* speak the language of Hotspur, Henry, and Hal—if he could adopt blank verse as his natural, rather than an occasionally comic style—he could be issued his visa into history. But from history, and especially the high history of *Henry V*, Falstaff is permanently alienated both factually and, we now see, verbally as well.

Allied to the stylistic aspects of the rejection is Hal's insistence on decorum in act and speech:

How ill white hairs *become* a fool and jester!
(line 52, my italics)

Reply not to me with a fool-born jest.
(line 50)

6. In his section on *Henry IV* in *Shakespeare's Prose* (Chicago and London, 1951), pp. 83–95, Milton Crane discusses the uses of prose and verse here and elsewhere; and Joan Webber also notes that Hal addresses Falstaff in blank verse for the first time when he rejects him—see "The Renewal of the King's Symbolic Role: From *Richard II* to *Henry V*," *Texas Studies in Literature and Language* 4 (1963): 530–538. Actually Hal has addressed Falstaff in blank verse twice before this, once in a "rejecting" moment at 1 *Henry IV*, 5.3.41–44, and once in his obsequy over Falstaff's still puffing "corpse."

And as we hear you do reform yourselves
We will, according to your strengths and qualities,
Give you advancement.

(lines 72–74)

"Becomingness," however, is meager fare for a fool and jester, who without a steady supply of the incongruous, the disproportionate, and the unbecoming will grow white-haired and very ill indeed. To require Falstaff to reform himself in the interests of decorum is literally to kill him off as a comic character. Similarly, to reduce his huge girth of styles to the single pattern of blank verse—to the corseted soberness of the Lord Chief Justice's speech, for instance, or to the prim Prince John's—would be to destroy Falstaff in the form in which we have so roundly known him.

Still, my point is that Hal is not entirely responsible for Falstaff's death; he merely finishes up a job that was begun after Shrewsbury by both him and Falstaff.[7] For when Falstaff abandoned theatricality for

7. I should mention that the argument usually put forward is that Shakespeare prepares for the rejection of Falstaff by making us judge him in advance. C. L. Barber says that in the early part of 2 *Henry IV* Falstaff "is constantly put in the position of answering for his way of life. . . . So during the first two acts we are again and again put in the position of judging him, although we continue to laugh with him" (*Shakespeare's Festive Comedy*, p. 215). However, I wonder if we could really continue to laugh with Falstaff if we were at the same time subjecting him to serious moral scrutiny, or vice versa. Yet surely, except for those who, like Prince John, drink no wine and hence remain sober-blooded, we do "continue to laugh with him." Perhaps, then, these callings-on-the-carpet are designed not to make us judge Falstaff but to substitute for our judging

realism and became not so much a character playing the role of actor as a character playing himself, much of him died. Perhaps the metaphor of the mask is more accurate here. Thus we would say that whereas in 1 *Henry IV* the mask of "Falstaff" was always on—so much so that the man did not wear the mask but *was* the mask—in 2 *Henry IV* the old, white-haired, disease-ridden, empty-pocketed fat man is separate from the Falstaff-mask. Only now and then does he put the mask on, and when he does we can see his veined eyes through the holes and his bad teeth through the paper lips. This apparition appears before Hal at Westminster, and he who once said "I know you all" now says "I know thee not, old man." He speaks the truth. He never knew the "old man" within the Falstaff mask, because in 1 *Henry IV* there was no old man, only the costumed stage figure of an old man with the mask of a jowly, debauched, white-haired clown, its expression fixed in a timeless rubbery grin of comic invulnerability. Now, however, the mask itself has grown tattered and ill fitting, and beneath the clown's bulbous nose is a real bulbous nose, beneath the white wig is

---

him. With such judges inside the play as the Chief Justice, Mistress Quickly with Fang and Snare, and that same young sober-blooded boy Prince John, what need is there of us as well? We are, by virtue of their judicial presence, released from our sterner responsibilities and permitted to indulge ourselves in holiday, secure in the knowledge that everyday and its unbending judgment will come soon enough with Hal's coronation. The following chapter, incidentally, takes up the matter of what we are led to expect in 2 *Henry IV* and how our experience of the play is governed by these expectations.

white hair: "How ill white hairs become a fool and jester!" And the clown's fixed grin disappears easily: "Master Shallow, I owe you a thousand pound."

If Hal looks through the Falstaff mask to see merely an old man he refuses to know, Falstaff attempts to see the young prince he knew—"my royal Hal," "my sweet boy"—and encounters instead an unfamiliar mask. For Hal is now wearing the mask of "Henry the Fifth" and denying to Falstaff, and to himself, the impulses and accents of his private person: "Presume not that I am the thing I was." From now on, role-playing, self-dramatizing, stagings of scenes, and manipulations of audiences, these theatrical functions pass out of Falstaff's keeping and into the king's. Performances controlled by Henry the Fifth are necessarily of a different order than those of Falstaff. Before turning to that issue, however, we need to look at the rejection of Falstaff from a different perspective, one that puts Hal in a less villainous light.

6

1 AND 2 *Henry IV:*

SUCCESSIVE FORM AND
THE REDEEMED WORD

If verbal statements were not condemned to proceed one at a time in lineal sequence this chapter would probably follow chapter 3, perhaps cramped into the margins or squeezed between the lines of chapters 4 and 5. I say this not merely to lament the obvious fact that criticism must limp the long way and shuffle to and fro in its attempts to choreograph Shakespeare's polysemous gambolings, but to bring the notion of sequence itself to the fore, where Shakespeare also brings it near the end of 2 *Henry IV*, especially in 4.5 when Hal "steals" and then lineally receives the crown. Before taking another glance at that scene, however, let me run through some commonplaces about visual and verbal forms.

One of the virtues of visual designs is that all of their parts are simultaneously available to the observer. Or at least they should be, according to Aristotle, who warns against overly large tragic plots on the visual analogy of an animal several miles long whose unity and wholeness could not be registered by the roving eye (*Poetics*, ch. 7). But given the proper magnitude, a visual design presents all of its aesthetic statement at once; all the parts are there simultaneously. Nevertheless, it cannot be experienced at once. Even in the case of a small painting, the eye must pass from detail to detail, though perhaps registering a blurred image of the whole as it does so. Because of this, there is a possibility of sequence in the experiencing of visual forms that might be exploited through clever arrangement. A painting might be designed to be "read" from left to right, foreground to background, top to bottom; a sculpture might be fashioned to lure the eye sequentially "through" or "around" the work somehow.

But the fact that all the parts of a visual design are simultaneously available to us, even though we do not experience them all simultaneously, ought to discourage the artist from banking very heavily on sequential viewing, especially if we are asked to follow a series of more than two or three items. However invitingly the painter or sculptor dresses up what is supposed to be the entranceway to his work, we may through ignorance, accident, or sheer contentiousness plunge in through the side window or the back door. Thus static spatial designs do not readily lend themselves to creating surprise and expectation—attitudes easily produced by lineal works like music and literature—and that most rudimentary product of sequential forms, suspense, seems difficult to generate by means of a spatial form and quite impossible to generate and then relieve.[1]

1. I suppose the "Ode on a Grecian Urn" might seem to testify to the ability of a spatial work, the urn itself, to arouse and subsequently to relieve suspense in at least the urn's versifying observer. The relieving of suspense, how-

Successive Form and the Redeemed Word

If static spatial forms sometimes do exhibit sequential features, as though striving to deny the limitations of their nature, lineal forms may return the
favor in various ways, depending on which features of
spatial forms they aspire to.[2] The sheer visualness of

---

ever, is accomplished not by some further development
of the urn's sylvan "history," not by its answering the
mysterious questions raised by its pastoral figures, but by
its suggesting to the observer-speaker that the beauty with
which its questions are posed makes answers unnecessary
(aesthetics obviates scientific inquiry). The relieving of
tension comes not from within, is not implicit in the urn's
form or figures, but from without, from the observer-
speaker's reflections on the relationship between beauty
and truth. In that sense the resolution is not much different from that involved when we come to terms with the
initially disturbing features of any creative work.

2. Of course emblem books and collections like Blake's
that utilize etchings as well as verse aspire to the best of
both expressive worlds, and in a more limited visual way
drama employs the stage as to some extent a "picture" of
its script. As a boy, Henry James was addicted not so much
to drama as to scenic portrayals in prose. He would devote
three quarto pages to verbal depictions of his scenes and
the fourth page to a visual illustration: "I thought, I lisped,
at any rate I composed, in scenes; though how much or how
far, the scenes 'came' is another affair. Entrances, exits,
the indication of 'business,' the animation of dialogue, the
multiplication of designated characters, were things de-
lightful in themselves—while I panted toward the canvas
on which I should fling my figures; which it took me longer
to fill than it had taken me to write what went with it, but
which had on the other hand something of the interest of
the dramatist's casting of his *personae*, and must have
helped me to believe in the validity of my subject" (Henry
James, *A Small Boy and Others*, quoted by F. O. Matthies-
sen in *The James Family* [New York, 1961], p. 76).

spatial works may give rise in lineal works to imagery, pictorial passages, descriptive detail; the material substantiality of spatial works may be imitated in sound through meter, rhyme, alliteration, and other repetitive devices. But I should think that lineal works might be particularly envious of the presentational fullness of the visual design, its capacity to "say" everything at once, instead of stringing it out tiresomely. A lineal work may want to telescope its ending back into its beginning, as *Finnegans Wake* so conspicuously does, or roundelays in music, so that all phases of its aesthetic statement are presented simultaneously. Meter has something of this effect. In verse there is normally a certain tension between the lineal thrust of statement and the repetitive return of meter. After the first metrical foot, as it were, there is no other; all subsequent sounds in an iambic poem are telescoped backwards into the first iamb, which says it all, as the first pentameter line does in a blank verse work. Or so they would if rhythmic variations did not intervene to create new developments.

In verse, statement normally overruns or outruns, or perhaps outfoots, meter. But even if statement slips its metrical clogs and escapes into prose it may want to loop back upon itself and grasp at the simultaneity of the visual. Conjunctions and adverbs like *however, yet, but, or,* and *moreover* are signals of an attempt to return to an earlier point in a sentence or argument and fill out the "picture" presented there, an attempt to acquire the presentational fullness of visual objects, which must seem to represent the truth of the case, the full truth, better than a lingering wandering, onthrusting, that is progressive, or more precisely developmental, though to be sure often repetitive, but nevertheless temporally successive mode of expression. But, as the previous sentence indicates, these attempts to go back and get it all said at once are inevitably self-defeating because the only way in which statements can go back is by going on.

The necessity of going on is not entirely unfortunate, however. In fact it may be the source of great power, particularly to the dramatist. For the static visual design, as I suggested, is at the mercy of the eye, whose penchant for wandering where it lists is notorious. Sequential forms in print—books and poems and articles—may enforce a certain discipline on the eye, but even they may be read out of sequence, as when the reader of a suspenseful narrative skips to the end to see how it comes out and then goes back, or more likely doesn't. But the dramatist, who in other respects is powerless to control the presentation of his work, is sovereign yet in this, that he reigns supreme over the sequence in which his work is experienced by the audience. To turn the argument in the direction of 2 *Henry IV*, 4.5, we may say that the "succession" depends on his royal will, which is to say on the royal Will. Because of this, time also falls under his sway. Unless we arrive at the theater late or depart early, Shakespeare decrees the precise amount of time we spend in the presence of his work—a prerogative denied the writer of printed literature, not to mention the artist of spatial forms. That is why, three times at the end of *The Tempest*, Shakespeare confidently equates the time taken by Prospero to work his wonders on his subjects with that taken by Shakespeare to work his on us. For once we enter his theatrical kingdom and relinquish the right to order our own experience, we too are the playwright's subjects.

Because of the nature of successive speech, our condition as theatrical subjects is indeed parlous. For one virtue of speech, as opposed to visual configurations, is that what is said can always be, if not quite unsaid, at least resaid—qualified, corrected, augmented, even denied at a later point. As a consequence, verbal forms are never fully defined until they have had their final say, the last word. Periodic sentences hold their meanings in stylistic suspension until the last instant. Jokes are merely aimless verbal oddities until suddenly invested with meaning by a punchline. So too with literary works. Dramatic forms are only latent —possible, probable, gradually perhaps inevitable, but still not actual—until their actions are completed, until the lovers marry and make our play a comedy or the king dies and confirms our fears of tragedy. For this reason we may find ourselves victimized by such lineal tricks as the *deus ex machina*. Finding evidence of bad faith in a painting or sculpture, we can turn quickly away without having lost a great deal. But by the end of a play we have banked heavily on the dramatist's integrity. If he breaks faith with us we stand to lose a large investment of psychic capital.

Probably in no other mode of artistic expression, then, is the bond between author and audience so obviously and crucially a formal one. If the play is to transcend the random disorder of life and achieve dramatic form, it must make good on its promises. The expectations the playwright arouses in his audience must be met and resolved, the debts he contracts must be paid. In such meetings and resolutions, with such payments, form itself comes into being.[3]

*

I said awhile ago that with the "succession" under his control the dramatist acquires regal powers. Actually his right to determine the succession implies that he is less a king himself than a divine kingmaker. It is in this kingmaking role that Shakespeare, looking before and after within the lineal succession of his own plays, decreed that *Henry IV* should succeed *Richard II* and that *Henry V* should succeed *Henry IV*. Surely that was how he originally envisaged the succession.

3. The notion of the debt contracted and subsequently paid off that I use throughout this chapter—and that Shakespeare uses throughout *Henry IV*—metaphorically expresses a conception of literary form held by Kenneth Burke some years back, as when he said "form is the creation of an appetite in the mind of the auditor, and the adequate satisfying of that appetite. . . . If, in a work of art, the poet says something, let us say, about a meeting, writes in such a way that we desire to observe that meeting, and then, if he places that meeting before us—that is form. While obviously, that is also the psychology of the audience, since it involves desires and their appeasements" ("Psychology and Form" in his *Counter-Statement* [New York, 1931]). By the same token, when Shakespeare makes such preparations, arouses such desires, and then, as at Gaultree Forest, brings them to nothing—that is a deliberate sabotaging of form. This chapter issues from my puzzlement about such apparently self-defeating willfulness on Shakespeare's part.

But in the kingdom of the theater, the course of history plays is no more comfortably assured than the course of history itself; and as it develops, *Henry IV* is succeeded not by *Henry V* but by *Henry IV, Part 2*. As chroniclers of Shakespeare's creative sequence, we need to ask ourselves what interrupted the playwright's succession.

This is a question to which various critics have addressed themselves under the heading of structure. What, they have asked, is the relation of Part 1 to Part 2? Are they one long play arbitrarily divided, as Dr. Johnson claimed, or two quite independent plays, as John Upton held, or one self-contained play with an unpremeditated sequel, as M. A. Shaaber argued, or what?[4] Without summarizing the succession of critical positions, let me quickly agree with Harold Jenkins, who in what seems to me the best treatment of this issue claims that "in the course of writing *Henry IV* Shakespeare changed his mind." He goes on:

> I am compelled to believe that the author himself foresaw, I will even say intended, that pattern which evolves through the early acts of Part 1 and which demands for its completion that the

4. Dr. Johnson's remarks appear in his notes to 2 *Henry IV*—see *Johnson on Shakespeare*, ed. Walter Raleigh (London, 1908), p. 124. He was responding to Upton's claim about the discreteness of the plays, which appeared in *Critical Observations on Shakespeare* (London, 1746), pp. 11, 41–42, 70–71. M. A. Shaaber's article is "The Unity of *Henry IV*," *Joseph Quincy Adams Memorial Studies* (Washington, D.C., 1948), pp. 217–227. His position is supported by H. Edward Cain in "Further Light on the Relation of 1 and 2 *Henry IV*," *Shakespeare Quarterly* 3 (1952): 21–38.

hero's rise to an eminence of valour shall be accompanied, or at least swiftly followed, by the banishment of the riotous friends who hope to profit from his reign. In other words, hard upon the Battle of Shrewsbury there was to come the coronation of the hero as king.[5]

But at some point well along in the play Shakespeare abandoned this plan. Why he did so, Jenkins does not say, but the result is an altered ending. Instead of having a preparatory function in the movement toward the death of Henry IV and the coronation of Hal, the battle of Shrewsbury is now expanded to become "a grand finale in its own right."

In our eagerness to come to this battle and our gratification at the exciting climax it provides, we easily lose sight of our previous expectations. Most of us, I suspect, go from the theatre well satisfied with the improvised conclusion. It is not, of course, that we cease to care about the fate of individuals. On the contrary, the battle succeeds so well because amid the crowded tumult of the fighting it keeps the key figures in due prominence. Clearly showing who is killed, who is rescued, and who shams dead, who slays a valiant foe and who only pretends to, it brings each man to a destiny that we perceive to be appropriate. We merely fail to notice that the destiny is not in every case what

5. Harold Jenkins, *The Structural Problem in Shakespeare's Henry the Fourth* (London, 1956), reprinted in slightly abridged form in *Discussions of Shakespeare's Histories*, ed. R. J. Dorius (Boston, 1964), pp. 41–55—the passage quoted is from page 51.

was promised. There is no room now in Part 1 to
banish Falstaff.

(p. 52)

And so, to complete his original plan, Shakespeare is
obliged to write Part 2, at the end of which Falstaff's
fate finally catches up to him.

Jenkins's interpretation is excellently conducted
and far more convincingly laid out than I can take time
here to indicate. However, in arguing that Shakespeare's unexplained change of mind worked him into
a structural corner where he was left insufficient room
to banish Falstaff, Jenkins turns a causal sequence backwards, I think. For if we ask why Shakespeare changed
his mind and hence the form of *Henry IV*, or as I put
it earlier, if we ask ourselves what interrupted the
Shakespearean succession, the answer is surely: a co-
lossal impediment, a huge hill of flesh. In the course of
writing his play Shakespeare discovered that he had
created, if not a monster of nature, a marvel of art—
a character of such immense comic vitality that he is
not only witty in himself but the cause that wit is in
other men, especially in the playwright. He is also,
Shakespeare could easily foresee, the cause that audiences were, and continue to be, in the theater. "Banish
such a character as this," Shakespeare must have
thought, "and where will I come by another?" For as
Dr. Johnson's adoring remarks point out, Falstaff is not
merely "unimitated" but "unimitable," a unique creation that beggars even Johnsonian description. No,
banish plump Jack and banish a word of dramatic op-
portunities and half a Globe of playgoers to boot!

So I set forth the obvious: that it is precisely be-

cause Falstaff's theatrical life is far from used up, as
Shakespeare perceived, that the form of 1 *Henry IV*
shifts in the manner Jenkins indicates. It is not that a
lack of dramatic space kept Shakespeare from banish-
ing Falstaff but that his desire to keep Falstaff unban-
ished caused him to occupy that space otherwise. How
he occupied it, in fact, may confirm this interpretation; for, pushed into improvisation by the master improviser himself, Shakespeare fashions a scene in which
his structural problems are given dramatic focus—act
5, scene 4. Instead of killing Falstaff off, he first pretends to do so—"here, you see, is what I might have
done, to your and my infinite regret, but presto!"—
and then underscores Falstaff's theatrical vitality by
having him pop up from death to declare himself a
counterfeiter, which is just what Shakespeare himself
has become as he fabricates his substitute ending. And
instead of a final rejection, Shakespeare brings about a
significant reconciliation. Falstaff is shown about to
destroy the form of *Henry IV* by revolting against the
rule of realism (as was argued in chapter 4), and then
Hal is shown patching up that form—as Shakespeare
himself is doing—by means of a permissive lie. Hal
accepts Falstaff's lie and even gilds it with one of his
own in order to reincorporate the rebel into the play so
that he can continue his theatrical life in the sequel.
Thus it seems that Shakespeare has written into the
new ending of *Henry IV* the reasons for its existence.
By such devices *Henry IV* becomes *Henry IV, Part 1*,
with its unanticipated successor in the offing, soon to
be entered in *The Stationers' Register* as "*the second
parte of the history of kinge HENRY the 1111th with
the humours of Sir IOHN FFALLSTAFF*" (significant

billing). The Lord of Misrule will reign a while longer, even at the expense of the legitimate dramatic succession.

*

It is not very auspicious that in conceding to the theatrical desirability of keeping Falstaff alive and clowning Shakespeare makes the last memorable scene in his play end with a lie, however glitteringly gilded. The stress at this point on the lie required to accommodate Falstaff may remind us that Shakespeare has, if not precisely lied to us, at least modified his "word." His word was pledged to us in the opening act, conveyed by means of Hal's "I know you all" soliloquy, which builds to the following conclusions:

> So, when this loose behaviour I throw off
> And pay the debt I never promised,
> By how much better than my word I am,
> By so much shall I falsify men's hopes.
> And like bright metal on a sullen ground
> My reformation, glittering o'er my fault,
> Shall show more goodly and attract more eyes
> Than that which hath no foil to set it off.
> I'll so offend to make offence a skill,
> Redeeming time when men think least I will.
>   (1 *Hen. IV*, 1.2.231–240)

Whatever inferences we may draw about Hal on the basis of his soliloquy—is he secretive, hypocritical, devious, merely rationalizing?—it is, I think, less what Hal says that is important than what Shakespeare says through him. The soliloquy reveals Hal's plot as interior dramatist and indicates that Falstaff has been conscripted into that plot without his knowledge. By the same token, however, Hal is himself conscripted into Shakespeare's plot without knowing it. As princely playwright, Hal says that his plot will capitalize on the tactic of the surprise reversal, an unexpected reformation of character as Hal pays the debt he never promised. But in the very act of saying he will pay the unpromised debt Hal makes a promise to Shakespeare's audience—or Shakespeare makes it through Hal—a structural promise that the form of the play will presumably redeem. Hal's plot may rely on surprise, which has an effect on the audience (Coleridge said) like that produced by the sight of a shooting star; but Shakespeare's plot, as Hal is at this moment guaranteeing, relies on expectation, which has an effect on the audience (Coleridge also said) like that produced by witnessing a sunrise. If Hal "knows" Falstaff and company and will awhile uphold their disorder, Shakespeare also knows Hal and will awhile uphold his plot, but only because it is so readily incorporated into his own.

Shakespeare's play on surprise and expectation here indicates that he is quite conscious of his control over the linear sequence of our theatrical experience. If we are subjects in his domain, he is anxious to set us at ease—though his imagery puts it differently, more humbly: it is he who is our debtor. What he says to us through Hal's soliloquy runs somewhat like this:

> I assure you, my gentle creditors—for so I hope you will be—that if you lend me your patience, not to mention your pennies, I shall entertain you most faithfully with this fat knight, his fiery opponent in the camp of honor, and the young Prince here. But that you may be entertained, let us look

first to your fears. For the perceptive among you will have noticed that this round villain Oldcastle has the same name as the character in the old play *The Famous Victories of Henry the Fifth*—a graceless comedy—and even after I rechristen him Falstaff, as I (and the Brookes) have it in mind to do, I fear you will still see resemblances to that play. But rest easy; I have no intention of foisting on you another *Famous Victories*, with its psychopathic Prince who yearns for his father's death, gets wildly drunk, engages in "a bloodie fray," is clapped in jail, in turn claps the Chief Justice on the ear, rushes to court with his madcap companions at news of the King's illness, beats on the palace door, and actually steals upon the King with a drawn dagger. No, young Hal here is not the man, nor is this the play. *Our* Prince's mind runs to reformation even before his body runs to riot, and in the perfectness of time he will banish much of himself and all of his fat friend, not quite as we would wish perhaps, but as a King must. Trust me in this, so that you, like the Prince, may give some rein to pleasure, knowing the end is measure and justice.

Hal's soliloquy gives us more than reassurance; it grants us the luxury of not having to judge Falstaff, because Shakespeare has given us his word as a dramatist that the judgment of Falstaff will emerge from within the play itself. Thus it controls our experience of the play, enabling us to enter the world of holiday uninhibitedly, without fear that disorder will pass from the Boar's Head Tavern into Westminster Palace.

So, banking on Shakespeare's word, we move with the play toward a moment when we expect Falstaff to say "Banish plump Jack and banish all the world" and Hal to reply in earnest "I do." But that moment does not arrive in 1 *Henry IV*. Instead, we are presented with a counterfeit ending at Shrewsbury featuring the death and miraculous rebirth of Falstaff. Not that we would have it otherwise: we will gladly take Falstaff on the hoof instead of embowelled. Yet the fact is that we have been fobbed off—brilliantly, persuasively, no doubt with our best interests at heart —but still fobbed off. Precisely as Prince Hal has been, who has had good reason to expect a royal reward for his day's service, and finds that he must defer to the fat knight. Like Hal, though, we countenance Falstaff's lie and the improvised ending, which is Shakespeare's lie. We will accept a structural IOU from the dramatist so long as Falstaff is reprieved. Let the dramatic succession go—we will have our sweet creature of bombast, the roasted Maningtree ox with the pudding in his belly.

*

So Shakespeare passes from *Henry IV* not to *Henry V* but to *Henry IV, Part 2*, which is to say he interrupts his dramatic succession and keeps a little life left in the waning Henry so that Falstaff can caper before us. And the capering will have to take the center of the stage because Shakespeare has run low on historical material, or perhaps on the invention that would put it to good use. Part 2 is not the successor to Part 1—there is no creative advance involved—it is its shadow, or as M. A. Shaaber says it is its carbon copy, or as G. K. Hunter says, citing the "parallel presentation of incidents" in the two plays, it is the second half of a dramatic diptych.[6] The shadow may have the form but hardly the substance of its antecedent body. From Shrewsbury Field to Gaultree Forest, from Hotspur to Pistol, from the tavern scene of Part 1 (2.4) to its parallel in Part 2 (2.4)—what a falling off was there! Hal's comments on his own "case" (fall), his tactic of playing the princely *eiron*, sums up the movement from Part 1 to Part 2 as well:

> From a God to a bull? A heavy descension! It was Jove's case. From a prince to a prentice? A low transformation! It shall be mine; for in everything the purpose must weigh with the folly.
>
> (2 *Hen. IV*, 2.2.192–196)

What is the purpose that weighs with such folly? Hal's purpose for his low transformation, as he told us in his "I know you all" soliloquy, is to astound and please his English audience with an unexpected high transformation when he becomes king. But Hal's weary, half-disgusted tones here and earlier in this scene hardly reflect the optimistic self-assurance of his "I know you all" soliloquy of Part 1. But, after all, why should they?—Hal has small reason to rejoice. Having risen to heroic distinction at Shrewsbury, he has been cheated of or at least obliged to share his battlefield honors, and now instead of receiving the crown he has sweated to earn he must defer his kingship for another play and go back to playing straight man to Falstaff again. It's enough to make a prince

6. M. A. Shaaber, "The Unity of Henry IV" (see note 4 above). G. K. Hunter, "*Henry IV* and the Elizabethan Two-Part Play," *The Review of English Studies*, n.s. 5 (1954): 236–248.

abandon the stage. In fact, that is precisely what he does for most of the play.

And what is the "purpose" that weighs with Shakespeare's "folly"? For the moment his purpose—to spend a play fooling with Falstaff for the entertainment of his audience—seems not to justify but to constitute his folly. As the existence of the play depends on lies—Hal's, Falstaff's, Shakespeare's at the end of 1 *Henry IV*—so its mode of existence *is* the lie. This is a play whose major action is the preparation for action, for a violence that never comes. The principal violence in 2 *Henry IV* is that which is done to words as they are torn free from facts and truth. Henry the Fourth, usurper of the name of king, is on the throne—or at least in the royal sickbed. Falstaff, usurper of Hal's honors at Shrewsbury, is "Sir John with all Europe." Prince John, official spokesman, lies to the rebels at Gaultree. Henry's pilgrimage to the Holy Land dwindles into a mortal pun in the Jerusalem Chamber. And prefacing all is Rumour, the harlequin figure of the Induction, "painted full of tongues," who asks "Why is Rumour here?" The answer is gross as a mountain, open, palpable: because expectations, lies, misconstructions, and bad faith govern not only the England of 2 *Henry IV* but 2 *Henry IV* also.

Political and social order within the state is inconceivable unless there is some assurance that expectations will be met, that words, promises, vows, oaths, contracts, treaties, laws, and so on will be honored. In 1 *Henry IV* the honoring of vows and the underwriting of truth were symbolized in Hotspur, the "king of honor." It is fitting therefore that Northumberland,

learning of Hotspur's death after hearing rumors of
his victory, voices the consequences to a nation of
Rumour's rule:

> Let order die!
> And let this world no longer be a *stage*
> To feed contention in a ling'ring *act*.
> But let one spirit of the first-born Cain
> Reign in all bosoms, that, each heart being set
> On bloody courses, the rude *scene* may end,
> And darkness be the burier of the dead!
> (1.1.154–160, my italics)

Hotspur dies, his conqueror Hal by and large disappears from the stage, Rumour ascends the throne, and
order collapses. With the defeat of his own expectations, Northumberland raises expectations in us; we
are promised a drama of civil butchery. But though
he can say that his "honour is at pawn / And, but
[his] going, nothing can redeem it," Northumberland,
he who lay "crafty-sick" while Hotspur honored his
commitment at Shrewsbury, goes not to Gaultree Forest but unredeemed to Scotland (2.3.7–8).

    Northumberland's speech, proclaiming the death
of order by means of dramatic metaphors, comments
not merely on the rebel cause but also on 2 *Henry IV*
and the disorder that attends unfulfilled expectations
in drama. In the next scene in which the rebels appear
we find an unusual stress on plotting, on the raising of
hopes, on prudent forecasting. All of this concerns
plotting a rebellion, of course, but since the rebellion
is the primary historical action in 2 *Henry IV* it also
concerns plotting a play. "It never yet did hurt," Hast-
ings says, "To lay down likelihoods and forms of

hope" (1.3.34–35). Bardolph replies with one of those long, unrealistic speeches which often indicate that Shakespeare is backing away from the immediate drama into metadramatic reflections *on* the drama. It is dangerous to plan a

> great work,
> Which is almost to pluck a kingdom down
> And set another up

without being quite sure that your confederates will pay their debt of men on the day of battle (1.3.48–50). Otherwise you will be "like one that draws the model of a house / Beyond his power to build it" (1.3.58–59). Prudent planning geared to one's ability to pay, that's the thing.

We can hardly read this without being reminded of what happens at Gaultree Forest later on. The rebels have apparently planned well enough; their promised men show up. It is Shakespeare who has drawn the model of a house beyond his power or desire to build it. In all the scenes focusing on the rebels, in the tavern scene in which Hal and Falstaff are called forth to the wars, in the court scenes where the king frets sleeplessly about the state, in the Gloucestershire scenes where Falstaff impresses soldiers to put down rebellion—in most of the play, that is, Shakespeare lays us down likelihoods and forms of hope that the plot of 2 *Henry IV*, like that of 1 *Henry IV*, is advancing toward a great battle that will resolve all issues. Yet these formal promises of combat, which constitute the playwright's word, degenerate at Gaultree into another kind of word, Prince John's lies—just as the potential combat between Falstaff and Colville of the Dale collapses

123

into a surrender prompted by Falstaff's lying reputation. At Gaultree, Prince John, who speaks for England and claims divine inspiration, becomes humorlessly, without the excusing inspiration of sherris-sack, the official state version of Falstaff—the Falstaff who is master of the disavowed word and the disclaimed debt, who, with his belly full of tongues pronouncing his own name, has become the embodiment within the play of the prologue Rumor ("painted full of tongues").

Why? Why should Shakespeare spend an entire play preparing, and announcing his preparations, for an action that never materializes? Of course Shakespeare is bound to history, and Gaultree Forest did turn out roughly in this fashion. But he was not bound to incorporate the battle into his play (a messenger could have reported it, for example), nor to give to Prince John the role historically played by Westmoreland, nor to marshal all his dramatic resources and direct them toward this abortive end. Having, like Rumour, stuffed our ears with false reports, has Shakespeare become infected with Falstaff's and Prince John's cynicism? Is he willing, with Northumberland, to let dramatic order die?

*

For the characters within the play one major expectation remains. It is voiced somewhat hysterically by the dying King Henry, who thinks he has had earnest of its fulfillment when Hal "steals" his crown:

> Pluck down my officers, break my decrees,
> For now a time is come to mock at form.

Harry the Fifth is crowned! Up, vanity!
Down, royal state!

(4.5.118–121)

Henry goes on at some length, calling up images of an
England given over to license and riot, and (as always,
it seems when Shakespeare describes the abandonment
of order) maligning wolves: "O thou wilt be a wilder-
ness again / Peopled with wolves, thy old inhabitants!"
(4.5.137–138). Henry's fears that "a time is come to
mock at form" echo Northumberland's anarchic "Let
order die"—at a point, after Gaultree, when civil disorder has just been quelled at the apparent expense of
dramatic form and order. If Henry's fears proved true
at the end of 2 *Henry IV*, then a time would indeed
have come to mock at form. For the notion of Henry
the Fifth as king of vanity, plunging arm-in-arm with
Falstaff from Westminster to Eastcheap—or, worse,
to Agincourt—is the one expectation we have been told
not to entertain. Shakespeare has repeatedly put his
dramatic honor in pawn by pledging to us that Hal's
long proposed reversal of character and rejection of
Falstaff will in fact come to pass. We have it on Shakespeare's word that form will not be mocked.

And yet up to this point in the play, form—that is
to say our expectations, which is the same thing—has
been mocked. But now we come to the scene in which
Shakespeare throws such unusual stress on the concept
of succession (4.5). At the end of chapter 3 I suggested
that this scene transforms an act of apparent usurpation into a sanctioned lineal descent of the crown from
king to heir apparent, and that this reinstitution of the

political succession implies a parallel reinstitution of verbal creativity as we move from Richard's monistic language of names to its successor, a language of lies but also of metaphors. Perhaps now, however, we are in a position to see that this scene also announces the recovery of a more immediate and dramatic kind of Shakespearean creativity and in so doing helps define the function and nature of 2 *Henry IV*.

Henry's reign, lingered out in Part 2, is construed by Henry himself as a mere marking of historical time, a putting down of the rebellious consequences of his usurpation of the crown:

> For all my reign hath been but as a scene
> Acting that argument. And now my death
> Changes the mode; for what in me was purchased
> Falls upon thee in a more fairer sort,
> So thou the garland wear'st successively.
>
> (lines 198–202)

Henry, as he and Hal both recognize, is merely the political bridge that Henry the Fifth must burn behind him, a sacrificial figure who takes the "soil of the achievement" into the grave with him so that Hal can look to the future (to Agincourt, for instance) instead of back over his shoulder as he tries to trammel up the consequences of usurpation.

Like Henry's reign, 2 *Henry IV* represents a marking of time until Shakespeare can "change the mode" and reinstitute his own dramatic succession. Its "argument" too has been the suppression of rebellion, the maintenance of order. Part 2 is necessarily a holding action. *Henry IV* can no more succeed *Henry IV* than

Bolingbroke can succeed Bolingbroke. It can only linger out the life that was in the earlier play while repeating its formal structure, its dramatic order. Shakespeare is engaged not in an advance but in a doubling back, not in creation but in re-creation.

Gaultree Forest seems to present a Shakespearean judgment on the form of 2 *Henry IV* much as the destructive entrance of Mercade does on the form of *Love's Labour's Lost*. The negotiations there reveal that the structure but not the substance of 1 *Henry IV* is all that survives in 2 *Henry IV*, that we have been witness to "a low transformation." Prince John's role at Gaultree, as he evidently sees it, is to preserve at any cost the political order of Henry IV. Shakespeare's role in writing 2 *Henry IV* is analogous—to preserve the dramatic order of *Henry IV* (Part 1) by maintaining a parallel presentation of incidents, a carbon copy of form. Prince John accomplishes his task by crafting the substance of a lie into the affable form of a truth, by extending to the rebels the letter of accord masking the spirit of vengeance. Shakespeare, as literally true to his word as Prince John is, brings his play to a point that corresponds to the battle of Shrewsbury in Part 1. And, as at Shrewsbury, Henry's order is upheld.

But at what price? Surely the fact of a low transformation is well advertised. Instead of Hal's proposal of single combat before the lines with Hotspur, instead of his later defeat of Douglas and saving of Henry's life, we now have Prince John's

My lord, these griefs shall be with speed redressed.
Upon my soul, they shall. If this may please you,

> Discharge your powers unto their several counties,
> As we will ours; and here between the armies
> Let's drink together friendly and embrace.
>> (4.2.59–63)

Instead of Hal's liberality with defeated enemies (not to mention triumphant friends!), his

> Go to the Douglas and deliver him
> Up to his pleasure, ransomless and free
>> (5.5.27–28)

—we have Prince John's "Strike up our drums, pursue the scattered stray" (4.2.210). And, by contrast, Prince John's piously generous "God, and not we, hath safely fought today" (line 121).

The cost of Shakespeare's retracing the pattern of 1 *Henry IV*, he seems to announce here, is nothing less than dramatic form. The old order survives, but emptily, and preserving it is seen to be at odds with the formal obligations imposed on the dramatist by the sequential nature of his art. He has put his audience, its expectations quite defeated, in a mood to ask of him, as Mowbray asks of John, "Is this proceeding just and honourable?" (4.2.110) and, with the Archbishop, "Will you thus break your faith?" (line 112). If he has not broken his faith with us, he has kept it only in the Prince John fashion, or in the way that Henry, arriving at "Jerusalem," keeps his vow to make a pilgrimage to the Holy Land.

*

The metradramatic implications of Gaultree Forest become comparatively explicit in 4.5 when Henry and Hal acknowledge the interim nature of Henry's kingship and the saving virtues of the succession. 2 *Henry IV*, also an interim and to some extent opportunistic venture, has a kind of inauthentic legitimacy like Henry's reign. It has the name but not the substance and vitality of its predecessor, not the formal integrity that comes when a work finds its way to an order of its own shaping. Having parasitically fed on a dramatic order already largely used up, it has called order itself in question. Northumberland's remedy is anarchic, "Let order die!" Falstaff's is predatory, "I see no reason in the law of nature but I may snap at him." Prince John's is cynically casuistic. Hal's response has been to withdraw from the general contamination and wait. He and his father now recognize that the present order must be transcended or gone beyond. *Henry IV* must be succeeded by *Henry V*, whose splendors will give a retroactive sanction to the cloudy dramatic interim, much as the glories of Henry the Fifth will retroactively sanction (or at least meliorate) the indirect crooked ways by which Bolingbroke met the crown:

> for what in me was purchased
> Falls upon thee in a more fairer sort.
> So thou the garland wear'st successively.
> (4.5.200–202)

Succession is all. What Shakespeare now appears to be banking on is the restoration of sequence. It is the nature of a lineal work that it may repeat itself, as 2 *Henry IV* has so weakly done; that its form is dependent on generating and fulfilling expectations in its audience, as 2 *Henry IV* has not done; and that its form is not fully established until the last word is delivered, as 2 *Henry IV* is preparing to do.

As Falstaff rides toward Westminster we know that expectations are bound to fail, but we are not precisely sure how. On the one hand, acting on the principle of the disclaimed debt and the broken word—the principle that dominates the play by means of Rumour, Falstaff, and Prince John—Shakespeare may renege on his structural promise as he did at Gaultree Forest and somehow accept Falstaff into Hal's graces. The ending of 1 *Henry IV* may come to mind; Falstaff reprieved, resurrected, rebelling, and finally enticed back into the play. On the other hand, Shakespeare may "falsify men's hopes" in the Prince Hal fashion. By having Hal reject Falstaff at Westminster he will demonstrate that we playgoers have misjudged *him* much as Hal's audience of disapproving Englishmen have misjudged their greatest king. Thus Hal and Shakespeare will redeem their loose behavior simultaneously, Hal redeeming time and Shakespeare redeeming his play when men think least they will.

We know of course which way Shakespeare chooses—has chosen from the beginning. "Let the end try the man," Hal told Poins (2.2.50–51), and Shakespeare apparently says to us, "Let the end also try the play." In a play so shot through with irredeemable words, acts, and characters we may hesitate to endorse last-minute redemptions. Reinstituting the succession does not quite make up for "all the soil of the achievement." Nor, knowing what comes after, are we entirely reconciled to going on. We can spare Bolingbroke well enough, but losing Hal, Hotspur, and

Falstaff to gain Henry the Fifth or *Henry V* is an expensive trade, no matter how vigorously we unfurl reminders of national destiny.

Still, Shakespeare's keeping a promise, his making even one word stand up, is something of an achievement in 2 *Henry IV*. The point is pressed on us when the payment of Shakespeare's and Hal's verbal and formal debt causes the rebuffed Falstaff to do what he seemed constitutionally incapable of doing: acknowledge a debt ("Master Shallow, I owe you a thousand pound" [5.5.76]) and maintain his word ("Sir, I will be as good as my word" [5.5.90]). In the Epilogue Shakespeare continues to play on the theme of the debt incurred, disregarded, and paid:

> Be it known to you, as it is very well, I was lately here in the end of a displeasing play, to pray your patience for it and to promise you a better. I meant indeed to pay you with this, which if like an ill venture it come unluckily home, I break, and you, my gentle creditors, lose. Here I promised you I would be, and here I commit my body to your mercies. Bate me some and I will pay you some and, as most debtors do, promise you infinitely: and so I kneel down before you—but indeed to pray for the Queen.[7]

7. I depart from the Folio text to present the first paragraph of the Epilogue here as it appeared in the Quarto. The Folio prints the clause after the colon—"and so I kneel down before you—but indeed to pray for the Queen"—at the end of the third paragraph of the Epilogue. I agree with the New Arden editor, A. R. Humphreys, when he says "The original form of the Epilogue was presumably the first paragraph only of the existing three" ("Introduction," xv [London, 1966]). Which means that at that time Shake-

In 2 *Henry IV* Shakespeare has, as he says, done what most debtors do, promise us infinitely—become, like Falstaff with Mrs. Quickly, an infinitive thing upon our score. Still, when the debt fell due at the end, he paid—and so earns his right to the humor of the Epilogue—though he missed some payments elsewhere, at Gaultree for instance. Perhaps we must bate him some—take Gaultree off his score—and he will, as with Falstaff here, pay us some. The rejection of Falstaff cannot redeem all the debts racked up by 2 *Henry IV*, even if we let the end try the play. But Shakespeare indicates in the final lines of the play proper that he has not finished paying, there is more to come:

Lan. I will lay odds that ere this year expire
We bear our civil swords and native fire
As far as France. I heard a bird so sing,
Whose music, to my thinking, pleased the King
(5.5.111–114)

It is through the succession, what is dramatically to come, that Shakespeare will be released from his debt —not by repeating past successes but by succeeding them with new forms, new orders. As experienced creditors, we may take leave to doubt that he can pay us in full with *Henry V*. But the dramatic succession from there on—which passes by lineal descent not to *Henry VI* but to *Julius Caesar*, who is succeeded by

---

speare had no intention of continuing the story "with Sir John in it," as the later addition to the Epilogue states. Evidently Falstaff's box office appeal continued in force, however, and Shakespeare was persuaded at least temporarily to write him into *Henry V*, later changing his mind, revising him out of it, but leaving a few unobliterated traces of his former presence—some lard upon the plain.

Hamlet, who is succeeded by *Othello,* and so on—that succession will warrant an infinite extension of credit to this most promising but sometimes late-paying playwright.

7

Henry V:

THE ACT OF ORDER

As argued in the previous chapter, *Henry IV, Part 2* is a static moment in Shakespeare's *Henriad*, a holding action in which the playwright repeats the form, though not the substance, of *Henry IV, Part 1*. 2 *Henry IV* does not so much succeed the earlier play as recast it, attenuating its order—the old order—to the point where, as Northumberland suggests, order itself might well die. In act 4, scene 5, however, Hal and his dying father together realize that the old order—the waning reign of Henry IV—has been merely a sacrificial interim that now must yield to national destiny. History must resume; Henry V must succeed Henry IV. Drama too must resume; *Henry V* must succeed *Henry IV*. Act 4, scene 5 releases England from the reign of its usurper king and Shakespeare's tetralogy from the paralysis of 2 *Henry IV*, which had usurped the place intended for *Henry V* in the dramatic succession.[1]

1. This is not to imply some sort of failure in 2 *Henry IV* as a play but only to acknowledge what has often been noted, that it is parallel in form to 1 *Henry IV*. Like most sequels, it is overshadowed by its predecessor, and of course the virtues of 1 *Henry IV* are extraordinary. But 2 *Henry IV*, is, nevertheless, a work of Shakespeare's dramatic maturity—rich in language and character, energeti-

Henry V is a king who "succeeds" in both senses of the word, both inheriting a crown and triumphing with it. As a play, however, *Henry V* has by no means triumphed with the critics. "Many people find *Henry V* offensive," Sigurd Burckhardt observes, "though they argue whether it is offensively foolish or offensively knavish. Was Shakespeare nationalist fool enough to believe such stuff, or was he theatrical knave enough to exploit it?"[2] Let me defer for the while the question of the play's "success" as triumph in order to consider its success as sequential advance. That it is an advance, a shaping of a new kind of dramatic order, is argued by its New Arden editor, J. H. Walter, who says:

> Shakespeare's task was not merely to extract material for a play from an epic story, but within the physical limits of the stage and within the admittedly inadequate dramatic convention to give the illusion of an epic whole. In consequence *Henry V* is daringly novel, nothing quite like it had been seen on the stage before.[3]

No wonder, then, Walter observes, that Shakespeare, after his epic invocation in the Prologue—"O for a

---

cally humorous, shrewdly perceptive of the machinations of political power—by no means the "pot-boiler" some critics have called it. (David Young ably defends the play against such charges in his introduction to *Twentieth Century Interpretations of Henry IV, Part II* (Englewood Cliffs, N.J., 1968), p. 1–12.)

2. Sigurd Burckhardt, *Shakespearean Meanings* (Princeton, 1968), pp. 192–193.

3. J. H. Walter, "Introduction," *King Henry V* (London, 1954), pp. xv–xvi.

Muse of fire . . ."—quickly grows apologetic about the
inadequacies of the theater to represent the manifold
of history. The same theme of apology runs through
all the prologues and the epilogue. Since history in its
"huge and proper life" cannot "be here presented"
(Prologue, Act 5), it must be re-presented, not in its
wholeness but in its "partness." A thousand men are
reduced to one man and "the accomplishment of many
years / Into an hour-glass" (lines 24, 30–31). The
technique is essentially metaphoric and, since metaphor requires an act of imaginative completion by a
reader, Shakespeare asks here not merely for his audience's indulgence but for their imaginative assistance
in creating the "tenor" of English history by means of
the "vehicle" of metaphoric theater. More specifically,
however, the technique is synecdochic, using the dramatic part to stand for the historic whole.

The relation of part to whole is a cardinal issue in
Henry V, for the illusion of epic unity that Shakespeare is seeking is sought also—and rather readily discovered—by King Harry in the political sphere. The
ideological basis for political unity is supplied by the
Archbishop of Canterbury's speech in act 1 about divine, natural, governmental, and military order (1.2.
183–220). The speech itself is curiously excessive to
the problem of defending England from the Scots
while Harry's armies are in France. Ultimately it is
decided to divide Harry's forces into four parts, leave
three in England, and take one to France. But this rather
obvious solution comes only after some thirty-four
lines by Exeter and Canterbury justifying such division
on the grounds of unity of purpose. Illustrations of this
kind of unity are drawn from music, sundials, archery,

the confluence of roads and streams, and most expansively from bees—"Creatures that by a rule of nature teach / The act of order to a peopled kingdom" (1.2. 188–189). In this Platonic perspective the emphasis is upon transcendence. Particulars are of no value in themselves; a man achieves fulfillment not by cultivating singularity but by submerging himself in a larger scheme. Self-servers like Bardolph and Nym will be brought down, to the full stretch of hemp, and even Pistol will be demeaned—that sorry stand-in for the Great Gormandizer must come at last to dine on leeks. On the other hand, through personal sacrifice and useful service, the individual transcends himself to become a functional part of the greater whole. Thus the Many, whether bees or barons, become the One.

Such an order—in which the individual part is justified by its relation to the whole—suggests the kind of synecdochic representation of historic whole by dramatic part to which Shakespeare calls attention in his prologue. Canterbury's speech surely addresses the problem of epic unity in drama as well as national unity in England, and we may well wonder, as Shakespeare appears to have done, whether honey-bees "teach the act of order" not merely to a peopled kingdom but also to playwrights who must people stages. In a play often called episodic, pageantlike, constructed as a series of tableaux, what principle of order does Shakespeare follow, what whole unifies his parts?

As an exposition of order in nature and society Canterbury's speech is perfectly orthodox; it dominates the conduct of the English throughout the play. National unity is achieved by inclusion and by exclusion —by incorporating the Welsh Fluellen, the Irish Macmorris, and the Scottish Jamy into the English cause, for example, and by eliminating the English traitors, the disobedient Bardolph and Nym, and ultimately the opposing French. The French are, of course, poor imitators of God's confluent order. In 3.5 their preparations for battle seem largely to consist of a roll call of titled names: "High dukes, great princes, barons, lords, and knights" (3.5.40–46). Harry can cite noble names too (4.3.51–55), but he can also give tribute to the worker bees and the cooperative hive:

> We few, we happy few, we band of brothers.
> For he today that sheds his blood with me
> Shall be my brother. Be he ne'er so vile,
> This day shall gentle his condition.
>
> (4.3.60–63)

It is true that Harry has not so much established a happy democracy here as introduced upward mobility into the Great Chain of Being. Even so, in contrast to the feudal French, he proposes a "gentling of condition" that is earned rather than inherited, a brotherhood with the king that is achieved not through shared bloodlines but through shared blood losses. Then, during the final act, after the harsh dialectics of combat, we are given a glimpse of a transcendent synthesis. King Harry and Princess Katherine are to lose their individuality and, "being two, are one in love" (5.2.389). Frenchmen and Englishmen are to lose their nationalities and mingle indistinguishably as members of God's international community (395–396), though we may take leave to doubt whether the conquering English are as anxious as the conquered French to dissolve all differences.

The demand for unity in England is fully honored by England's new king, whose own personality is a microcosm of the nation in this regard. Everyone has lamented the loss of Prince Hal in King Harry, nearly as much as the loss of Falstaff in *Henry V*, for the newly crowned king's famous "I know thee not, old man" seems also to have meant "I know thee not, young prince." At any rate, the various-minded Hal, who moved gracefully between the worlds of court, tavern, and battlefield, who could speak prose as well as verse, who could say "I am now of all humours that have showed themselves humours since the old days of good-man Adam to the pupil age of this present twelve o'clock midnight," has been succeeded by King Harry, single-mindedly pious, militant, even ruthless. Victories can not do without victims, and the victims add up: Falstaff ("I know thee not, old man"), Lord Scroop and his fellow traitors ("Touching our person seek we no revenge, / But we our kingdom's safety must so tender" . . .), the citizens of Harfleur whom Harry's armies will ravage ("What is it then to me. . . . What is't to me. . .?"), Bardolph of the lantern nose ("We would have all such offenders so cut off"), the French prisoners at Agincourt ("Then every soldier kill his prisoners"), and finally Katherine, who though only coyly resistant is nevertheless part of the spoils of war.

So thoroughly has Hal disappeared with Falstaff from *Henry V* that Una Ellis-Fermor has claimed it is futile to "look for the personality of Henry behind the king; there is nothing else there. . . . There is no Henry, only a king."[4] This is both true and untrue. It is true

4. Una Ellis-Fermor, *The Frontiers of Drama* (London, 1945), p. 45. Ms. Ellis-Fermor feels that Shakespeare grows

that, as Alvin Kernan says, our "difficulties in understanding the King are intensified by the almost total
absence from the play of speeches in which Henry
speaks as a private man, directly revealing his own
feelings," and that Harry "lives in the full glare of
public life."[5] But it is not true that the crown never
leaves Harry's head. Shakespeare is quite clear about
that on the eve of Agincourt when he has Harry tell
Bates:

> For, though I speak it to you, I think the King is
> but a man, as I am. The violet smells to him as it
> does to me; the element shows to him as it doth to
> me; all his senses have but human conditions. His
> ceremonies laid by, in his nakedness he appears
> but a man . . .
>
> $\qquad$ (4.1.105ff.).

Public office and private man are for Harry the reverse
of what they were for Hal. As part of his sun-cloud
strategy Hal suppressed his princeliness, making his
office—or his training for office—private, and gave

---

dissatisfied with this bloodless King Harry and in later
plays, especially *Antony and Cleopatra*, makes a plea "for
the supreme claims of the individual spirit," which becomes
impoverished when it surrenders to the demands of public
life (p. 53). I agree that Harry's public office takes a heavy
toll of his private personality. But Shakespeare is not quite
the romantic Ms. Ellis-Fermor makes him out to be. The
autonomy of the individual spirit does not fare too well in
Coriolanus .

5. Alvin B. Kernan, "*The Henriad*: Shakespeare's Major
History Plays," in *Modern Shakespearean Criticism*, ed.
Alvin B. Kernan (New York, 1970), p. 272. Kernan has an
excellently conducted discussion of the entire tetralogy.

public expression to the wayward young man. Intending to prove "better than [his] word," he has, as Henry V, become so. Harry the man is now kept private, suppressed in favor of Harry the king, who is nearly always on public display. In keeping with the theme of unity, the private man is subsumed by the public office. As for his motives, they are the motives of a king who consults England's welfare rather than his own feelings before rendering decisions. Not for himself but for the nation Harry declares war, executes traitors, threatens Harfleur, refuses ransom, orders prisoners killed, gives credit for the victory to God, and marries Katherine.

The very unity of Harry's character as king—the lack of self-division, conflict, and the ironies these give rise to—provokes dissatisfaction, though more often in critics than in audiences. Moody Prior puts it well:

> The misleading notion of a sly Machiavellian Henry V growing out of *Henry IV* is an understandable product of unsympathetic critics attempting to find a consistent center for this character. Since it is hard to believe in the paragon, it seems sensible to look for the smart operator. There is, one might more properly contend, too little of Prince Hal and his father in the character. All the rich if sometimes contradictory and even unpleasant possibilities which have been built up over two plays are largely set aside in the interest of the hero of Agincourt and the myth of the spotless Christian king who upon his coronation was made new. The reader is not so completely persuaded of the miraculous change as the bishops, and in consequence Henry V turns off more people than does

his father, the political man who knew himself for what he was.[6]

Harry's personality is united under his political office, and his conduct in office is designed to unite the nation in accordance with Canterbury's speech on order. As Harry's piety testifies, God stands in relation to Harry's well-ordered character as He does also to order in England, for God has been Englished by Canterbury's rhetoric. God created order in nature, the English and Harry imitate it and triumph, the French fail to do so and predictably suffer.

6. Moody E. Prior, *The Drama of Power: Studies in Shakespeare's History Plays* (Evanston, Ill., 1973), p. 331. Prior cites one of the play's unsympathetic critics, L. C. Knights, as saying, "It is one of the curiosities of literature that *Henry V* should have been seen so often as a simple glorification of the hero-king," and replies, "It is also one of the curiosities of literature that the heroic view of the play can in our day be undercut with the air of an uncontroversial judgment" (p. 311).

While I sympathize with those who find Harry stuffy, chauvinistic, overly pious, rhetorical, and even on occasion Machiavellian, I agree with Prior that to seek "below the surface of the text to discover a 'truer' one, which is at odds with it" is to warp the play, for "We are thus required to regard *Henry V* as a work of sustained irony, with the inevitable result that the idea of Henry as 'the mirror of all Christian kings' appears to be a gigantic put-on which, in its own day, presumably only Shakespeare could have been on to" (pp. 313–314). I do not see how such a play could be realized in the theater, whereas the Laurence Olivier film takes the surface of the text straight and is eminently playable. I do not suppose that Shakespeare was entirely happy with Harry, but I think he may have regarded him as an ideal English king without feeling that he was an ideal dramatic character (see note 9 below).

The Act of Order

Cast in military form, Canterbury's confluent order appears as a united English army mowing down the French nobility. Cast in dramatic form, it would appear as a play all the parts of which yield to a unifying principle. Taken metadramatically, Canterbury's speech might be seen as an apologia for the playwright who, claiming a kind of divine authority, nationalizes his literary themes, suppresses internal dissent, and tailors his characters and actions to a partisan pattern. And this is partly the case. Shakespeare the English dramatist has to some degree imitated Harry the English king in suppressing private feeling in favor of national interest. He too achieves unity through inclusion and exclusion. If Harry has rejected Falstaff at Westminster, thus killing his heart, as the Hostess claims, Shakespeare has done the dramatic equivalent, writing Falstaff out of *Henry V* (despite his promise in the Epilogue of *2 Henry IV* to "continue the story, with Sir John in it") and literally killing his heart offstage. The epic-heroic mode is no country for unemployed highwaymen. Falstaff's burlesques of a prince who in the *Henry IV* plays was himself given to burlesque were harmless enough. But with the prince turned king, and pious to boot, those flouts and parodies would give us pauses that Shakespeare's play cannot abide. So too with the remaining low-life characters. If Harry eliminates the traitorous Grey, Scroop, and Cambridge, Shakespeare diminishes in his turn the comic rebels Bardolph, Nym, and Pistol. If they survive Falstaff, as though to inherit his role as parodist, they are granted a toothless parody at best. No sooner have they mimicked Harry's "Once more unto the breach" address at Harfleur—in a scene of uninspired humor—

than Fluellen arrives to pummel them into battle and the Boy lingers on to satirize the would-be satirists. Their villainies stem, the Boy claims, from a failure to match words with deeds—"For Pistol, he hath a killing tongue and a quiet sword" and "For Nym . . . his few bad words are matched with as few good deeds" (3.2.35–42). As a result their burlesque of the main plot succeeds only in degrading themselves. Instead of being made to seem foolish, Harry emerges as the one man whose words are more than matched by his deeds, as he declared they would be from the beginning: "By how much better than my word I am, / By so much shall I falsify men's hopes" (1 *Hen. IV*, 1.2.233–234). In the remainder of this scene, having excluded the three self-serving parasites, Shakespeare underscores unity by inclusion with the three representatives of England's habitually churlish border nations—the Welsh Fluellen, the Irish Macmorris, and the Scottish Jamy—who, though contentious enough with one another, are united in their desire, as Jamy puts it, to "de gud service" against the French (3.2.123).

All that remains, then, now that the English are in harmony, is to do in the French. History having made the English victory a foregone conclusion, Shakespeare can busy himself to make it glorious. It is not enough that the French lose at Agincourt; they must also deserve to lose. Hence the Dauphin is made supercilious and arrogant, and the French in general, especially in 3.7 and 4.2, are presented as fatuously insolent. In them feudal chivalry has degenerated into a mannered doting on trivia, of which the Dauphin's sonnet in praise of his horse is emblematic.

Finally, having protected Harry and England

from within by aggrandizing those who are "with" and either eliminating or degrading those who are "against" the national cause, Shakespeare takes pains to indemnify the epic-heroic mode against misinterpretation from without. In the Induction to 2 *Henry IV* Rumour announced himself as running up and down England sowing dissension of understanding. In a play so prefaced, false expectations, ironic double meanings, and mistrust will afflict not merely the characters but the audience as well. But Rumour is succeeded in *Henry V* by the Chorus, whose name in itself implies musical unity and whose dramatic function is to secure unity of interpretation. We are told in unambiguous tones what to expect in this play and how to respond to it. As an English audience, we are told to identify with, to admire, and to yearn for the lost glories of Henry's reign.[7]

Not only does the Chorus encourage unity of interpretation, it also helps create unity of structure in the play itself by building narrative bridges between the five acts whose discreteness has prompted from critics such adjectives as episodic and tableaulike. This

7. For unsympathetic critics, the Chorus is rather awkward and must somehow be discounted. Harold Goddard, who regards the play as covertly antiwar, does this rather easily by claiming, "Through the Choruses, the playwright gives us the popular idea of his hero. In the play, the poet tells the truth about him. We are free to accept whichever of the two we prefer" (*The Meaning of Shakespeare*, vol. 1 [Chicago, 1951], p. 218). But of course one is hardly "free" to choose between "the popular idea" and the poetic "truth." The problem here, as Prior notes, is that Goddard obliges us to overturn the normal dramatic convention which assigns truth to choruses, prologues, and the like.

structural unity to which the Chorus contributes reinforces the internal thematic unity of the play, which is
so rigorous in behalf of the English, so disturbingly
suggestive of a "God's on our side" chauvinism, that
many critics have sought evidence of Shakespearean
irony. For how could he either believe, as Burckhardt
says, or exploit such stuff? How could he—by killing
off Falstaff and degrading the comic subplot characters, by making the French ridiculous, by making us
view everything through the patriotic eyes of the
Chorus—how could he stack the dramatic deck so
blatantly?

*

The issue is larger than chauvinism and the question of Shakespeare's patriotic beliefs or theatrical op-
portunism. We encounter here an old critical problem
that new critical attention has brought into sharper
focus. If literary works consist of a marriage between
parts and whole, which of the partners to this marriage
must defer to the other? Should priority be given to
unity and wholeness—to Apollonian order, Aristotelian form, Hegel's synthesis, Ransom's universal,
Tate's intension, Frye's archetype? If so, how much
Platonic oneness can the work permit without converting its marriage into a bleak domestic tyranny of the
whole over the parts? On the other hand, will not too
great a complexity of parts—Hegel's dialectical conflict, Empson's ambiguity, Brooks's paradox, Warren's
impurity, Wimsatt's hateful contraries, Krieger's existential chaos, and so on—dissolve all order and unity
in the work? How much Dionysiac dancing and rebellious individuality can the work permit without con-

verting its marriage into a domestic insurrection of parts against whole? In this direction madness lies; in that, an arid sanity.

Chaos, strife, and irresolution come cheap. Any literary neophyte, mind boggling like Bottom's with inexpressible dreams, can strew a page with slices and shards of irreconcilable "life." Order is another matter. To cast the clutter of raw experience into even a trivial, third-hand, sentimental order takes a measure, however small, of literary skill. By its nature order must be imposed, and its price, the price of unity in the work, is necessarily the autonomy of the parts, of the division and strife that make for internal complexity. This unifying, overdone, as I have said, is from the purpose of art; and so, to save the work from the grey homogeneity of an order too repressively imposed, we welcome, invite, cast about for intramural complications. But, on the other hand, to prevent the work from becoming a dizzying reproduction of life's disorder— Yvor Winters's "fallacy of imitative form"—we concede that these intramural complications must be resolvable.

With the notion of resolvable complications we seem to have got safely out of this winding dark wood of poetics. But alas, as Murray Krieger reminds us, resolvable complications come not by the grace of Manichaean chance but by authorial design, no less so than the preordained structure of meaning in the most rigid of allegories.[8] For to introduce resolvable com-

8. For a compendium of the difficulties encountered in this connection by the organistic school of criticism in recent years, see Murray Krieger's excellent "Recent Criticism, 'Thematics,' and the Existential Dilemma" in *The*

plications the writer must load his artistic dice and call upon all his skill to disguise that fact. Instead of earning or achieving an order, instead of allowing a new order to emerge from the dialectical ordeal of the creative process, the writer will merely impose upon the work a preexistent order. And yet, what remedy? The literary dice are either loaded or they are not loaded; there are no degrees in between, such as their being only "slightly" loaded. If the writer plays for truth with loaded dice, he is patently dishonest. If he does not, he abandons the literary game to the randomness of chance. On the one hand he is not an honest artist, on the other he is not an artist at all.

I think Shakespeare was aware of these problems, indeed, this dilemma, and that we can see him exploring it in *Henry V*. Faced with the obligation of writing *Henry V*, in fact, he could hardly avoid such issues. For a play in which "this star of England" is to be studied at its zenith makes more than ordinary demands on its author. Shakespeare knows, for instance, that he is bound by history. Not *enslaved* by it —he can collapse history's four dauphins into one for his purposes—but bound by it nevertheless, and willing to admit as much in his prologues, as when the epilogue refers to "Our bending author [who]

Tragic Vision (New York, 1960), pp. 228–268. For further developments of the same theme, see his "Platonism, Manichaeism, and the Resolution of Tension: A Dialogue" in *The Play and Place of Criticism* (Baltimore, 1967), pp. 195–218, and the opening chapter of *The Classic Vision* (Baltimore, 1971), pp. 3–51. My sense of the literary relations of Apollo and Dionysus is heavily in debt to Krieger's formulations of the problem.

hath pursued the story." Moreover, he knows that he is bound by his own immediate literary history, the three preceding plays in *The Henriad*. History alone would have authorized him to conclude *Henry V* with, say, Harry's death and funeral as readily as with Agincourt and a marriage. But the *Henry IV* plays have guaranteed us that *Henry V* will exhibit sovereignty in success, ending not with death but with triumph and a sense of national fulfillment. And, finally, Shakespeare knows that he is bound by his audience and the nationality he shares with them. How he presents Harry and his England depends less on his own inclinations than on the expectations of an English audience who may not know the details of history but are steeped in awe for the mythical magnificence of Harry and his times.[9]

Having given hostages to English history, to his own tetralogy, and to the expectations of his English audience, Shakespeare might well have felt that writing *Henry V* was less an exercise in creative freedom than a discharge of obligations. Thus he seems to have written into the play a self-justifying rationale, a speech by the Archbishop of Canterbury emphasizing obedience to higher laws, self-sacrifice, all the virtues of the "act

9. My suggestion here that Harry and his England, that the play itself, owe as much to Shakespeare's audience as they do to the dramatist is confirmed by the Chorus throughout. If the ultimate reality of *Henry V* is achieved not on stage but in the imagination of the audience, as the Chorus keeps insisting, then the audience is at least partly responsible for the creation of this nationalistic drama. Shakespeare has written the play to the audience's specifications and relies on their imagination to bring it to fulfillment.

of order." Sanctified by the cause of national and dramatic unity, the play eliminates all dissension and advances toward Agincourt under God's banner.

But at this point Shakespeare seems to have suffered doubts. In any event, it is at this point that he inflicts doubts upon the previously self-assured King Harry. On the eve of Agincourt, when Harry goes disguised among his men, the foot-soldier Williams raises the question of royal responsibility and the rightness of the English cause in France:

> But if the cause be not good, the King himself hath a heavy reckoning to make when all those legs and arms and heads chopped off in battle shall join together at the latter day and cry all, "We died at such a place." . . . I am afeard there are few die well that die in a battle, for how can they charitably dispose of anything when blood is their argument. Now if these men do not die well it will be a black matter for the King that led them to it, who to disobey were against all proportion of subjection.
>
> (4.1.140ff.)

Williams asks, in effect, "Are my services to the king consistent with my obligations to God?" If they are, well and good; if they are not, the king must answer for it, since I am bound to his service.

We know what Richard's answer would have been: "For every [enemy] . . ./ God for his Richard hath in heavenly pay / A glorious angel" (*Rich. II*, 3.2.58–61). Service to a Divine Right king is service to God, and no soldier, however bloody his employment, need fear for his soul. We know too what Canterbury's answer would have been: "The English order is God's order, the English king is God's king, and the English war is God's war."

But Harry does not even begin to answer in this fashion. The gist of his reply—which is long, consistent, well illustrated, and quite beside the point—lies in one sentence: "Every subject's duty is the king's, but every subject's soul is his own" (4.1.185). Williams seems reassured, but he has small reason to be. At issue are not the private sins each soldier totals up in the general business of living—from that point of view, every subject's soul is indeed his own—but rather those sins he specifically commits "when blood is their argument," when he is, in the present case, piling up legs and arms and heads to support Harry's claims in France. From this standpoint, each subject's soul and duty are inevitably the king's responsibility, and the question comes back, "Is the king's cause also God's cause?"

That, however, is precisely the question Harry avoids. The reason for this avoidance is not far to seek. In his speech on Ceremony immediately following the departure of the soldiers Harry demythologizes kingship rather as Falstaff did honor at Shrewsbury. In contrast to Canterbury's thesis about God and His divine order standing surety for the king and his well-regulated state—in effect, the old Ricardian "divine right" view of politics—King Harry confesses that there is nothing inherently majestic about majesty. "Place, degree, and form" are not ways in which men participate in divine order but merely instruments of political expediency "creating awe and fear in other men" and lending dignity to the exercise of power (4.1.263–264). Then Harry addresses a prayer to the

"God of battles" asking Him to "think not upon the fault / [His] father made in compassing the crown" (lines 310–311) and citing at length his own contrition for Richard's death and efforts in his spiritual behalf.

Despite Harry's regal confidence up to this point, we now see that he is uneasily aware that he owes his kingship not to God but to his usurping, regicidal father. Perhaps this uneasiness has been with him earlier. For if God *had* made him king, if he were graced with the Divine Right legitimacy of a Richard, Harry would not have had to rely on Canterbury to sanctify the invasion of France ("The sin upon my head, dread sovereign!" [1.2.97]). Nor would he have had to make others responsible for his decisions: the Dauphin and his father for the war (1.2. 284–288, 2.4.105–109), the English traitors for their punishment ("The mercy that was quick in us but late, / By your own counsel is suppressed and killed" [2.2.79–80]), the citizens of Harfleur for atrocities done them ("What is it to me, when you yourselves are cause" [3.3.19]), and the foot-soldiers for the perils of their souls.[10] As God's vicegerent, King Harry would legitimize his ventures by the act of announcing them. But how Harry's credit stands in heaven, heaven alone knows. Instead of inheriting Divine Right from

10. In his *Political Characters of Shakespeare* (London, 1945), John Palmer notes Harry's need "to justify his conduct . . . and to evade responsibility for his actions" (p. 237), as does Charles Mitchell in "*Henry V*: The Essential King," in *Shakespearean Essays*, ed. Alvin Thaler and Norman Sanders (Knoxville, Tenn., 1964), pp. 97–103. Mitchell also has some good observations about Harry's lowering himself to the level of his men as a means of rising toward true kingship.

Henry IV, he has inherited mere Ceremony—"titles blown from adulation"—a showy but sorry substitute.

If Harry's regal insecurities account directly for the priests singing and the poor praying for Richard's soul, they also account for Harry's general oversupply of piety, his almost automatic qualification of every stated intention with a "God willing" or "God before" or "But this lies all within the will of God." These are symptoms not merely of routine religious deference but of Harry's quasi-fallen royalty. If the king cannot claim to speak *for* God as His appointed agent, he had better speak *to* Him as His devoted appellant.[11]

Harry's speech on Ceremony and his prayer to the God of battles have no effect upon the English, who of course remain as united as before; but they do call into question the aesthetic and thematic unity of *Henry V*. However foreordained the outcome of Agincourt may be from the standpoint of the audience, Shakespeare takes unusual pains to assure us that from Harry's perspective there are no guarantees whatsoever. God will bring no legions to Agincourt in support of the beleaguered English. In His divine wisdom He may know in advance how the plot turns out—who wins, who loses, who's in, who's out—but in His divine inscrutability He keeps His intentions shrouded. Up until now it has seemed that God's role was that of a participant who had chosen a side to defend. Now it appears that He is in

11. In "The Renewal of the King's Symbolic Role: From *Richard II* to *Henry V*," *Texas Studies in Literature and Language* 4 (1963), Joan Webber notes this distinction between Harry and Richard. She observes that Harry can to some extent remedy his inability to speak for God by acquiring the ability to speak for all his people.

the role of a judge who will render a verdict after re-
viewing the military, and presumably the moral and
spiritual, evidence on both sides.[12]

With God's withdrawal from overt partisanship,
what had seemed a sure thing takes on the character of
a genuine contest, a true trial of the English cause. That
means, for Harry and the English, an element of risk.
The French, who are going to die at Agincourt but who
cannot know that, take no risks beforehand; they ride
the odds and their sleek horses toward an obvious
victory. The English, on the other hand, most of whom
are not going to die at Agincourt but who cannot know
that, ponder on St. Crispian's Eve the dreary likelihood
that their souls as well as their lives are in peril, and
then soberly risk both on the morrow.

And the king whom they follow at such risk, he

12. Sigurd Burckhardt argues that by having God render
His verdict only after the battle, instead of siding with the
English all along, Shakespeare has sought to play down
the sense of complacent chauvinism in the play—see *Shakespearean Meanings*, pp. 193–194. My reading of the play
finds God apparently on the English side until the eve of
Agincourt, when Harry is suffused in doubt, then evidently
withdrawn from partisanship until after the battle, when
we discover that he has somehow been present and influ-
ential after all.

Chauvinism is merely an especially obvious example of
authorial partisanship. An author rolls the kettle drum
more quietly in any work, if not for England's glory, then
for that of God, love, individualism, thrift and hard work,
joy of life, artistic freedom, or professorial pay hikes. The
question is how willing he is to submit his thesis to the
dialectical ordeal and to allow its claims to be modified by
the struggle.

risks most of all. First, of course, his life. Refusing to avail himself of kingly privileges by accepting ransom, as Williams had feared he might, Harry hazards his life as extremely as his men do theirs: "Bid them achieve me," he cautions the French herald, "and then sell my bones" (4.3.91). Second, he risks his title, not only to France but to England as well, as he did not understand when he cried "No king of England, if not king of France!" (2.2.193) God, we know, conferred kingship on Richard; and Bolingbroke, God knows, conferred it on himself, substituting Ceremony for Divine Right. With no claim to Divine Right and with no trust in Ceremony, Harry is afflicted with royal doubts. For if he remains tainted by his father's usurpation and regicide, then he is an impostor, and the English order descending from God is a fraud. If so, then Harry risks not only life and title but, as Williams feared, the lives and souls of all his soldiers as well. That most awesome risk Harry accepts as part of his own trial: "We must bear all."

Thus at Agincourt Harry redeems from hazard not only his own life, and the lives and souls of his men, but English kingship too, which has been in pawn since Richard's reign. Instead of Richard's inherited Divine Right, however, Harry acquires an earned human right to the crown, gained through ordeal by combat, "in plain shock and even play of battle" (4.8.114). On the day of battle his royal authenticity is plainly evident. If at Shrewsbury in 1 *Henry IV* the English sovereign was unrecognizable amid the (other) counterfeits dressed in his coats, at Agincourt no man walks in the king's coat but the king himself. Harry may pass unrecognized in Erpingham's cloak on St. Crispian's Eve, but on St. Crispian's Day every man knows who the King of England is.

At Agincourt King Harry also redeems the playwright Shakespeare from the charge of artistic despotism. As England and Harry's armies have banded together in self-righteous confidence of God's partisanship, so the play *Henry V* has been thematically unified by an act of order imposed on it by its partisan playwright. With God inside the play and Shakespeare outside it both bent on being fully English, *Henry V* exemplifies that tyranny of whole over parts, Apollo over Dionysus, thesis over antitheses, that we spoke of earlier. Or so it seems. From our present perspective, however, we can see that if Shakespeare framed Canterbury's speech on order as a justifying rationale not only for military unity in England but for an overbearing thematic unity in *Henry V* he at some point came to regard that speech with suspicion. Thus he subjects the Archbishop's routine recipes for national efficiency to a shrewd critique by the distraught King Harry, and in doing so he introduces an element of thematic dissension into his previously untroubled drama. What had seemed an uncontested whole is now challenged by a part, the very scene in which Harry's legitimacy is challenged by his fears of divine disfavor.

By rendering Harry's doubts so vividly at this point, Shakespeare in effect causes God to withdraw from apparent partisanship—and that emblemizes Shakespeare's own withdrawal from partisanship as omnipotent author, at least his withdrawal from the kind of naive, unexamined partisanship that seems to have characterized him thus far. Later on, as we know, when the battle is over, Harry will claim that God's "arm was here," that God was partisan after all. And we know too that Shakespeare's arm was certainly here, even though, like God, he seems to have announced his withdrawal. But if he has not totally withdrawn from the literary engagement—and of course how could he?—he has withdrawn from apparent chauvinism into a more sophisticated partisanship, making an honest playwright of himself, and an honest God of God, by bringing before us the very issue of honesty in art. From a too easy concept of literary order he wrests a new kind of order, tested in action and opposition, the dramatic ordeal by combat.

Harry undergoes his ordeal too. If his deepest fears hold true, then his royal legitimacy is no more valid than the gauds and trappings of office—mere Ceremony—and he is on his own. Say he is—what then? Harry has his look into the abyss, and what he sees there he takes in reasonable stride. If he cannot look to divine aid in battle, he will look to himself and his ragged followers. The battle is not won through divine interference but in familiar human ways— through courage, discipline, cooperative effort—and, to be sure, in familiar inhuman ways, through the proposed slaughter of French prisoners. His methods are no more legitimized in advance than is his kingship; they earn legitimacy in action, by proving successful in England's cause. The king will cut the throats of his prisoners if necessary, because he knows that God will not cut them for him—witness the ineffectual Richard calling in vain for angelic legions. So long as God voices judgment only after ordeals by combat, the king must do as he can—and find in his success a declaration of divine will:

> O God, thy arm was here
> And not to us, but to thy arm alone,
> Ascribe we all!
>
> (4.8.111–113)

We need not look for irony here, suspecting a hypocritical attempt to sanctify a dubious cause and a vicious victory with claims of divine support. The Chorus assures us in the Prologue to act 5 that Harry's piety is genuine: "Being free from vainness and self-glorious pride," the king gives "full trophy, signal, and ostent / Quite from himself to God." If we want hypocrisy, we need only remember Prince John's declaration after the nonbattle of Gaultree Forest: "God, and not we, hath safely fought today" (2 *Hen. IV*, 4.2.121). Not until Agincourt—not since Richard cast down his warder at Coventry, preventing the contest between Bolingbroke and Mowbray—has God had an opportunity to try the English in authentic combat. We may also remember that the price of Prince Hal's giving full trophy, signal, and ostent for the killing of Hotspur to Falstaff at Shrewsbury Field was a gilding lie. The price of giving credit for Agincourt to God is not a lie but, rather, a humble truth, an admission that the king is not that mortal splendor described by Shakespeare long ago, in the opening lines of 1 *Henry VI*, where Gloucester says of Harry:

> England ne'er had a king until his time.
> Virtue he had, deserving to command.
> His brandished sword did blind men with his beams;

His arms spread wider than a dragon's wings;
His sparkling eyes, replete with wrathful fire,
More dazzled and drove back his enemies
Than mid-day sun fierce bent against their faces.
What should I say? His deeds exceed all speech.
He ne'er lift up his hand but conquered.

(1.1.8–16)

Before this image of the king girt in the awesome robes of Ceremony ordinary men, whether friend or enemy, might well grow pale. But this is not the role Harry plays after the battle of Agincourt. Giving the honors to God, he is content himself to speak of wearing Fluellen's Welsh leeks on Saint Tavy's day "for a memorable honour," to commemorate not his own but his forbears' victories in France (4.7.95–109). And in keeping with his conception of the English as a band of brothers, he is also content to acknowledge his common ties with Fluellen: "For I am Welsh, you know, good countryman" (4.7.110).

Shakespeare's intention in this is not to diminish Harry's royalty but to indicate its source. In plain shock and even play of battle Harry has earned God's approval, and with it he has earned, not so much a new as an old and long-neglected concept of royal order. Ideally the English king derives his authority from God above and his subjects below, his own function being to mediate between the two. Richard, claiming his authority exclusively from on high, disregarded the downward direction of royal sway, lost touch with the commons, leased out the very land itself. Shakespeare makes a point of distinguishing Harry from Richard now by having Fluellen echo a famous speech by the dead king:

Not all the water in the rough rude sea
Can wash the balm off from an annointed king;
The breath of worldly men cannot depose
The deputy elected by the Lord.

(*Rich. II*, 3.3.54–57)

Unlike Richard, Harry has not been elected by the
Lord. He has had a corporate majesty founded on
shared English culture, English aspirations, English
blood. Thus Fluellen says, "All the water in the Wye
cannot wash your Majesty's Welsh plood out of your
pody, I can tell you that" (4.7.111–113), and adds:

> But Jeshu, I am your Majesty's countryman, I care
> not who know it. I will confess it to all the 'orld.
> I need not be ashamed of your Majesty, praised be
> God, so long as your Majesty's an honest man.

To which Harry replies, "God keep me so!"

Kingship, it is clear, has not descended on Harry;
he has risen to it. But he has not risen to it in his
father's fashion, Bolingbroke of the supple knees and
usurping mind, whose overeager "In God's name, I'll
ascend the regal throne" provoked Carlisle's righteous
"Marry, God forbid!" (*Rich. II*, 4.1.113–114). If Richard owed all to heaven, and Bolingbroke all to himself,
neither held full title to the crown. But Harry descends
to the level of his soldiers and rises with them to
heights of Agincourt, earning God's endorsement in
the process. The divine and temporal dimensions of
royal authority thus coalesce in English kingship as
they have not done since before Richard's time.

And, we must add, as they will not do for very
long in Harry's time. Only for a brief moment, a "small
time," as the Epilogue reminds us, does this star of

England give off an authentic royal glitter. If, in the metaphoric way of things, that implies that Shakespeare's act of dramatic order is no more enduring than Harry's, then we need to consider that order more closely yet.

8

Henry V:

ENGLISH, RHETORIC,
THEATER

The most difficult roles in Shakespeare are assigned to Oberon and Ariel, for the latter is ordered by Prospero to "be subject / To no sight but thine and mine" and Oberon is obliged by Shakespeare to turn to the audience and announce "I am invisible." *Henry V* has a role of similar difficulty. Although God does not appear in the list of characters He nevertheless appears in the play. Or does He? When Agincourt is safely won, Harry says:

> O God, thy arm was here;
> And not to us, but to thy arm alone,
> Ascribe we all! When, without stratagem
> But in plain shock and even play of battle,
> Was ever known so great and little loss
> On one part and on the other? Take it, God,
> For it is none but thine!
>
> (4.8.111–117)

Agincourt presents us with the "plain shock and even play of battle"—that is, it is a genuine contest—and yet "God, thy arm was here"—that is, it is not a genuine contest, for if God's arm was here, it was here in behalf of the English. Somehow God manages to enact a paradox of partisan impartiality. Perhaps the most that can be said is that God has been discreet. He has made Agincourt as genuine a contest as possible, not by abdicating His judgmental throne, but by eschewing ostentatious involvement. He has supplied no omens of victory to Harry, no portents or signs, offered no ghostly comforts in response to Harry's prayers, brought no legions into the field. Like Harry doffing regal Ceremony to go among his troops on the eve of Agincourt as a mere man, God gives over divine Ceremony and appears at Agincourt, if not as a "mere" God, at least as an unobtrusive one. So far as the audience can see, at any rate, Harry and the English are on their own.

To be present and yet invisible may come easily to gods and fairy kings—not so for dramatists. However commendable it might be for the playwright to remain impartial and divinely aloof from the internal factionalism of his work—even "paring his fingernails," as Stephen Dedalus would have it—he cannot help being present, at Agincourt or London, in the Forest of Arden or on the plains of Philippi. Like God, however, his presence may be either blatant or subtle. He can impose his dramatic order as conspicuously as Shakespeare does in Canterbury's speeches, blazoning his Englishness in an English cause; or he can aspire to a more genuine contest by generating complications, doubts, thematic oppositions—authentic antitheses against which his thesis must make its way. Shakespeare, I have argued, does what he can in this regard. Having loaded the dice to begin with, he does his best to unload them later. By compelling Harry to do battle in mortal doubt of God's inclinations, by holding God's judgment in abeyance until the dust has settled and the blood congealed, Shakespeare strives to achieve the dramatic equivalent of an ordeal by combat refereed by a concerned but distant God. In consequence, the English victory is both a divine gift—"O God, thy arm was here"—and a human achievement—"in plain shock and even play of battle." But the achievement comes first. Thus as Harry moves toward an earned kingship, *Henry V* moves toward an earned unity, making good its right to be so totally English.

More than that, perhaps, for we might want to argue that the play earns the right not merely to be English but also to be *in* English. At the end of the play we have a grand spousal of persons and nations, the political version of an overarching divine order, but of course behind the rituals of international harmony is poised the mailed fist of English nationalism.[1] By the same token, the linguistic version of divine order would be a marrying language that brings French and

1. Katherine, for instance, is not won over by the blandishments of a courtly lover—"I cannot so conjure up the spirit of love in her that he will appear in his true likeness," Harry tells Burgundy (5.2.315ff.)—but rather conquered by the siege of a soldier-king: "She is our capital demand, comprised / Within the fore-rank of our articles" (5.2.96–97). The French are obliged to remember that Harry is titled not merely *Roi d'Angleterre* but also *Heritier de France*. Thus when Burgundy, acting as though the forthcoming marriage were a private affair unrelated to national treaties and the past military engagements, conventionally remarks that love is blind, Harry sets the issue in its proper perspective: "It is so. And you may, some of you, thank love for my blindness, who cannot see many a fair French city for one fair French maid that stands in my way" (5.2.343–346).

English under the same verbal roof, a unifying Esperanto presided over by God, best maker of all marriages. But there is no such language at the end of *Henry V*, and in its absence the King's English will serve. Indeed, it has served all along. Up until Katherine's English lesson in act 3, the French have all spoken English, as of course they must in an English play. Yet precisely because they must, the fact that they do passes largely unnoticed. In act 3, scene 2, where Jamy, Fluellen, and Macmorris convene to quarrel, Shakespeare asks us to observe that the dialects of Scotland, Wales, and Ireland may rasp and clash against each other but still address themselves to the English cause in harmony. However, while we watch the play advance toward a great military engagement between England and France, a test of dominance, we are not likely to realize that from the moment they have begun to speak the French have already suffered total defeat from Shakespeare's all-conquering English language. The first words spoken by the French king are "Thus comes the English will full power upon us" (2.4.1). He might with equal truth have said "Thus comes *English* with full power upon us," since by the all-compelling grace of an English playwright King Charles is unwittingly gifted with his enemies' speech. At Shakespeare's Agincourt there can be little hope of success for the French when even their battle cries must be issued in English.

I may seem to be making too much of what is simply an unavoidable necessity of English drama, a theatrical convention without which the play could not play. After all, the French in *Henry IV*—not to mention Greeks, Romans, Danes, Bohemians, Italians, in other plays—also speak English without being pursued by a cry of critics. Why seems it so particular with *Henry V*?

Henry V raises this linguistic issue primarily by means of Katherine's language lesson in an act 3, which is related to the general problem of partisan impartiality discussed earlier. Here again the dramatist plays the partisan, forcing the King's English upon both his play and the French, just as he Englishes divine order and makes straw men of his French characters. This Englishing of things, which happens whenever an author marshals his literary forces toward a predetermined victory, appears from one standpoint to be a dishonest stacking of the dramatic deck, but from another to be the indispensable price of artistic order, form, and unity. Parts, if they are to be parts, must be subdued if the whole is to be whole. And what could better illustrate the necessity of wholeness than the language in which a work is to be presented? If English speech did not unify *Henry V*, Bacon's "second curse" of man, Babel, would descend on the theater, rendering the play unintelligible through a clash of competing vernaculars.

So we concede, a bit unhappily, that the playwright must stack his linguistic deck no less than his thematic one and thereby incur the charge of dishonesty. Yet perhaps he need not be totally dishonest. At the very least he can avoid being an out-and-out knave by practicing his low dramatic shifts with a certain openness. He can confess to his audience that beguilement and dissembling are his stock in trade. Dramatic conflicts, he will remind us, are by nature recalcitrant; they will not resolve themselves of their own accord. If the playwright merely sets down on the fields of Agincourt a band of ragged and starving English, the French will swallow them whole. Christian history needs God's aid, English drama needs the English playwright's.

I argued earlier that Shakespeare raises this issue when he figures the withdrawal and return of the partisan playwright in the withdrawal and return of a partisan God. A truly high-minded, impartial God should not aid the English, but somehow does. An English playwright should not, in all honesty, aid the English, but, in all practicality, he is obliged to. Now, with respect to language, Shakespeare makes a similar point, announcing what he is artistically doing, what he cannot help doing. He introduces, *before* Agincourt, a scene in which the French princess takes a lesson in English speech—as though it were foreordained that Katherine's French must in the future give place to Harry's English.

Of course it *is* foreordained: history will not have it otherwise. In dramatizing this fact by means of the language lesson, even before the battle whose outcome will produce Katherine's marriage to Harry, Shakespeare underscores a larger fact: that he has compelled the French to speak Harry's English throughout the play. Through Katherine's English lesson Shakespeare addresses his audience somewhat as follows: "Let us be open with one another. The judicious among you will observe that Katherine will need no English if the French win at Agincourt. *If* the French win at Agincourt, then my play will contain, in this scene of the language lesson, a conspicuous irrelevance, an un-Aristotelean superfluity, as Ben Jonson will be quick to inform me. But of course I will not let the French win at Agincourt, because they *did* not win at Agincourt. And I will not let them speak French in my play, regardless of what they spoke in history, because the backward among you—glovers' sons from Stratford and the like—cannot understand French, let alone write it. So if I have not been quite fair to the French, at least I am being fair to you by exposing my dishonesty. However, let us not speak of dishonesty in this matter, but rather of how remarkably well I have instructed these haughty French, that they speak English, if not, my lords, as well as you, at least as well as I."

With something of this kind of openness Shakespeare becomes as honest as the theater will permit, and in this sense he earns the right to couch his play in English, especially during the final act. There we see Katherine's French yielding to Harry's English; for he, despite a few courteous assays at French, can find truth only in his native tongue: "Now, fie upon my false French! By mine honour, in true English, I love thee, Kate" (5.2.236–237). It is entirely fitting that a king who spent an unprincely youth learning all the dialects of England, who could "drink with any tinker in his own language" (1 *Hen. IV*, 2.4.20), who studied "his companions / Like a strange tongue" (2 *Hen. IV*, 4.4.68–69), and who learned his lessons so well that "when he speaks, / The air, a chartered libertine, is still" (*Hen. V*, 1.1.47–48)—that a king who has acquired such a command of English should subject all other accents and languages to its strict dominion. The round of oaths to be sworn at the end of the play (5.2.398–402) will be sworn, we can be sure, in English. The French will yield their words to the English conqueror even as they have yielded them to the English playwright from the beginning. What has been imposed from without, by Shakespeare, has been earned from within, by Harry

*

Henry V ends with mention of this round of oaths whose purpose is to bind a man and a woman in marriage and two nations in peace. Shakespeare might have left it at this, ending on a note of triumph and reconciliation. Instead, however, he adds an Epilogue in which he reminds us that Harry's triumph was short-lived. His successors not only broke the peace he so laboriously earned but also "lost France and made his England bleed" (line 12). Given the stress in the final act upon the triumph of English as well as of *the* English, it is not merely the peace that is subverted by Shakespeare's Epilogue but also the language in which that peace is framed—in which the entire play is framed. It is as though Shakespeare, not entirely satisfied with *Henry V*, advertises in his Epilogue the impermanence of his achievement. The medium of dramatic expression has earned, it seems, only a short-term legitimacy. If these inferences are justified, we shall need to look more closely at the parallels between language and kingship.

Let me recapitulate. The breakdown of an ontological language in *Richard II* brings into divided focus both the lie and the metaphor as verbal symbionts. The *Henry IV* plays center in a fallen language whose once time-honored truths have been called in cynical doubt by a world governed at the top by the lying king at Westminster and at the bottom by the lying knight at Eastcheap. The young Prince Hal seems to accept the lie—not his father's kind, claiming to be more than he is, but his own kind, claiming to be less than he is —until he can wring from it a royal truth. More accurately, he begins with the appearance of a lie. What he has actually embraced is the doubleness of metaphor rather than the duplicity of the lie. If metaphor earns its truth by disguising itself as a lie, by claiming the name of another concept which it is not, then Hal makes his way to kingship metaphorically, by claiming the title of wastrel prince. This strategy, his descent into the clouds of Eastcheap in *Henry IV*, must pay off royally in *Henry V*—and of course does. Truancy miraculously issues in sense of duty, apparent self-indulgence as pious self-sacrifice. Once again, however, Harry finds himself confronted by metaphoric doubleness. He is not the perfect fusion of person and office, thing and name; he is not Richard II, the sacrosanct king of God's choice, but a mere man. On the other hand, he is not an outright lie, an illegitimate usurper of kingship; he is not Henry IV but a king by direct lineal descent. Lacking credentials from God, he who once played the wastrel prince must now play the regal monarch. So young Harry plays King Henry V, not without a certain histrionic self-consciousness, until he can be assured of his title at Agincourt.

To play the king is to play the actor, for the king must have many roles in his repertoire. He must be able to play Henry VI, listening to the Archbishop and remaining oblivious to what the Church stands to gain from war with France. He must be able to play Richard III, affable and guileless as he springs his trap on the traitors. And Tamburlaine, crying down atrocities on the citizens of Harfleur. And Hotspur, covetous of honor at Agincourt and blunt-spoken soldier wooing Katherine. And as the learned Fluellen reminds us, he must play Alexander, killing his friend Cleitus at least figuratively, "for there is figures in all things." In these roles Harry acts marvelously well, and the militant English road company for which he stars prospers apace.

Now to militant kingship the parallel in language is militant speech—that is to say, rhetoric, the dominant verbal style in *Henry V*. Rhetoric in Harry's employ has not yet become, as it did in the sixteenth century, the language of ostentation, all gawds and tassels, but remains primarily functional and combative.[2] Even when defined as the art of persuasion, rhetoric is a martial employment of words, its object being to conquer its verbal enemies through argument. And since conquest, as we have seen throughout *Henry V*, demands the ruthless subordination of individuals to the general cause, it follows that in the language of conquest words will be valued not in themselves but as instruments of political policy. "Turn him to any cause of policy," Canterbury says of the reformed Harry, and

> The Gordian knot of it he will unloose,
> Familiar as his garter; that when he speaks
> The air, a chartered libertine, is still,
> And the mute wonder lurketh in men's ears
> To steal his sweet and honeyed sentences;

2. In *The Presence of the Word* (New Haven and London, 1967), and especially in his chapter on "The Word and the Quest for Peace," Walter Ong discusses the close relationship between rhetoric and combat.

So that the art and practic part of life
Must be the mistress of this theoric.

(1.1.45–52)

The "sweet and honeyed" aspect of Harry's speech does not suggest rhetorical floweriness so much as the beehive theme of political order in which all parts serve the whole—as the royal honey of the king's language feeds men's ears, or as the "art and practic part of life" serves the "theoric" of policy. And to be sure, words in rhetorical service have something of the worker bee about them. Their job is not to glitter but to get things done. Thus Harry's rhetoric is servanted to action. In its most strident employment, in his pre-battle speeches, we have the Word as adrenalin. "Stiffen the sinews, summon up the blood," he cries before Harfleur (3.1.7); and after delivering his St. Crispian speech at Agincourt he concludes, "All things are ready, if our minds be so" (4.3.71). Rhetoric readies the mind, the mind readies the body, and a few unpromising English bodies, desperate with patriotism, go among the French like reapers.

However artificial, as in the considered hysteria of his exhortations before Harfleur, or bumbling, as in the near antispeech of his wooing of Katherine, Harry's speech accomplishes its rhetorical aims: it works. His stumbling French in the wooing scene reminds us that if he is not well-schooled in Katherine's language he most certainly is in his own. His studies of English in all its varieties and in all its classrooms, from Falstaff's taverns and highways to Hotspur's battlefields and Henry IV's court, have of course been also a studying of England herself. Through this self-imposed education Harry has made the King's English a composite of the speech of all England. As a result, the easy synecdoche by which the English king becomes "England"—as when King Charles commands his nobles to "Bar Harry England, that sweeps through our land" (3.5.48) —has in this king's case a more than usual claim to truth. Although Harry is careful to distinguish his ordinary self from his extraordinary office, as in the speech on Ceremony, the high office nevertheless confers its magnitude upon him. The play's almost obsessive concentration on the rhetorical figure of the king—on Harry's voice addressing his courtiers, his soldiers, the French, Katherine—presents us not with the self-singing Richard II, nor with the multilingual name-trumpetings of Falstaff, but with the self-transcending language of corporate majesty. With all ideolects gathered in this King's English, Harry has become a linguistic version of H. C. Earwicker in his role of "Here Comes Everybody"—the personification of a manifold but unified Respublica.[3]

*

Yet despite this air of success in Harry, there is that note of transitoriness in the Epilogue, an implication that Harry's and Shakespeare's achievements are fleeting. Why Shakespeare chose to end on that note becomes clearer if we return to the Chorus and con-

3. In "The Renewal of the King's Symbolic Role: From *Richard II* to *Henry V*," *Texas Studies in Literature and Language* 4 (1963): 530–538, Joan Webber emphasizes Harry's graduation from selfhood to statehood as he comes to speak less for himself than for England. Alvin B. Kernan also holds this view—see "*The Henriad*: Shakespeare's Major History Plays," in *Modern Shakespearean Criticism*, ed. Alvin B. Kernan (New York, 1970), pp. 245–275.

sider, as a parallel to the rhetorical issue, Shakespeare's preoccupation with the theatrical means at his disposal.

Henry V is surely the most self-conscious, even the most apologetic, of Shakespeare's plays. In the person of the Chorus the dramatist explores, exploits, but most of all laments the drawbacks of theatrical presentation. How can this "cockpit hold / The vasty fields of France," convey armies back and forth across the Channel, or telescope the historical accomplishments of decades into "an hourglass"? These, one notes, are visual rather than verbal problems. They would not arise if Shakespeare were writing an epic poem, as many have wished, instead of an epic drama. They do not arise, for instance, in such word-dominated histories as the *Henry VI* trilogy or even *Richard II*. In those plays he is concerned less with the nature of the stage than with that of speech. But now, with the Word fallen into disrepute, he addresses himself to the nonverbal dimensions of his art. If truth no longer resides in language, to be borne on speech to the expectant ears of his audience, then it must be conveyed to their eyes—though, alas, by the implausible makeshifts of theater: "Yet sit and see, / Minding true things by what their mockeries be" (Prologue, Act 4). Imparted by such scapegrace means, truth becomes something of an embarrassment. When Agincourt is sadly abridged to "four or five most vile and ragged foils / Right ill-disposed in brawl ridiculous" (Prologue, Act 4), Shakespeare is not apt to speak about drama holding the mirror of truth up to nature. What he does speak of again and again, however, and always disparagingly, is the purely functional nature of theater. Visual enactment is not a mimetic illusion of historical realities but an expedient, a device devoid of truth in itself, rather shabby beside the glories it depicts, indeed a mockery.

Yet the theater is not wholly without value and truth. The theatrical mockeries Shakespeare laments are analogous to the trappings of kingship that the troubled King Harry debunks on St. Crispian's Eve. Under the head of Ceremony, the royal stage properties—

> the balm, the sceptre, and the ball,
> The sword, the mace, the crown imperial,
> The intertissued robe of gold and pearl,
> The farced title running 'fore the King,
> The throne he sits on, [and] the tide of pomp
> That beats upon the high shore of this world
> (4.1.277–282)

—may be "thrice-gorgeous," but at bottom they exist merely to aggrandize the king and to create "awe and fear in other men." That the ceremonies of kingship have no inherent truth is an admission Harry makes, to be sure, only in private soliloquy. However, his conduct at Agincourt, where he makes his "farced title" an authentic title, is consistent with his soliloquy. On the field he earns his kingship, not by robing himself in Ceremony and thus distancing himself from his awed followers, but by putting off Ceremony and addressing his soldiers as coequals in the martial enterprise: "For he that sheds his blood with me / Shall be my brother" (4.3.61–62). Only by donning the leather and mail of an English soldier does he earn the "intertissued robe of gold and pearl" of a true English king. Thus it is not the charismatic Harry who triumphs at Agincourt but "We few, we happy few, we band of brothers" (4.3.60).

Like King Harry, Shakespeare recognizes the frailties of his own dramatic office, and if there is a Falstaffian ring to Harry's debunking of Ceremony, so is there in Shakespeare's choral apologies for the debasements of theater. In chapter 4 we saw Falstaff rising from apparent death and threatening to secede from *Henry IV* insofar as the play purports to be a realistic illusion of historical life. This internal uprising, which momentarily split the play into a mimetic dimension occupied most prominently by the "dead" Hotspur and an artistic-theatrical dimension occupied most fully by the live Falstaff, was put down by Prince Hal, who alone inhabited both dimensions. Now, in the choral prologues of *Henry V*, Shakespeare has elevated Falstaff's revolt against the play into an official principle of the play. Over and again the Chorus makes Falstaff's divisive point about the purely theatrical and inadequate nature of what sets itself up as true history. Falstaff, nervously debating how dead Percy really was and how genuine his own pretence to death, said in effect to the audience, "I am the only true man here, since I confess that the play is a sham. The others, who pretend to be real, are counterfeiters and liars." Now it is Shakespeare who takes this line. The theater, he admits, has its limitations. One begins with that. Ben Jonson keeps insisting that we cannot shift scenes from England to France, squeeze Agincourt into a narrow theatrical O, or roll out the whole story of Harry's reign in a scant three hours. Not, at any rate, if we want to keep mimetic faith with reality.

And Ben is absolute for mimesis. If he could, he would resurrect Harry and his fellows so that, playing themselves, they could reenact history before our eyes. Well, to be sure, that has its attractions:

O for a Muse of fire, that would ascend
The brightest heaven of invention,
A kingdom for a stage, princes to act,
And monarchs to behold the swelling scene!
Then should warlike Harry, like himself,
Assume the port of Mars; and at his heels,
Leashed in like hounds, should famine, sword, and fire
Crouch for employment. But. . . .

(Prologue, Act 1)

It is, as Fluellen might say, an honest "but." Instead of attempting to foist theatrical illusions upon his audience in a sixteenth-century forerunner of epic cinema —"on-site filming with a cast of thousands!"—Shakespeare plainly acknowledges the limits of theater. Calling up the past to enact itself again is past the size of dreaming. For that original production God was the dramatist, but now we must make do with substitute playwrights sharked up from Stratford, partisan men given to the native tongue. God, best maker of marriages, is also best maker of reality; it is no part of dramatic wisdom to enter the lists with Him. How He manages His mortal and unruly materials toward providential ends defies understanding; how He frames His historical plot and yet leaves his actors freedom of will is sheer bafflement. *This* playwright, the Chorus keeps reminding us, operates otherwise. He deals of necessity in visual shifts and verbal craft, in disguises, techniques, beguilements. Whatever the credulous may think, to the discerning, this playwright's hand, unlike God's, is everywhere apparent; his wonders are performed not mysteriously but brazenly.

In short, this playwright works less like God shaping existential dramas than like a king fashioning plays of state—like King Harry, for instance, who has his repertory of political illusions to call on, who relies on Ceremony to move the minds of his national audience, and who is conscious of the lack of inherent legitimacy in his methods and status. And therefore, as King Harry calls upon his followers to aid him as coequals at Agincourt, so the playwright Shakespeare calls upon his theatrical followers to aid him in recreating Agincourt. Indeed, in asking his audience to "eke out our performance with your mind" (Prologue, Act 3), he invites them to join with him as coauthors of the play. The theatrical victory that follows is, like Agincourt, the product of a collaborative enterprise. The unity of English spirit on the battlefield is mirrored by the unity of English minds in the theater.

This victory—so truly theatrical in being achieved by the collective imagination of playwright, actors, and audience—marks the distance Shakespeare has come from the self-containment, the purely individual sovereignty of the lyric-narrative poet. It is his plainest admission of a truth he has grown to recognize more clearly from play to play—that the passage from poetry to drama involves a loss of creative independence, a sacrifice of self to the dramatic office that is analogous to the sacrifice of self to the political office made by King Henry.

*

One would like to stop on that note of dramatic triumph—but must, like Shakespeare, add an epilogue. With the fall of a language instinct with truth and value, a language envisaged in *Richard II*, Shakespeare has passed in the *Henry IV* plays through a period in which language seems entirely corrupt, a multitudinous lie, and on in *Henry V* to rhetorical speech, in which words acquire pragmatic value as instruments of action.[4] Rhetoric as a response to the fall of language parallels Harry's reign as a response to the fall of kingship. That is, just as Harry, lacking Divine Right sovereignty, earns his title to kingship through an ordeal by combat at Agincourt, so rhetoric, lacking the automatic sovereignty of poetry, earns its keep in action, substituting for inherent validity an achieved validity. Moreover, this conception of rhetoric as a pragmatic use of words has its analogue in Shakespeare's stress upon the theater as self-erasing technique—the purely instrumental makeshift by which the truths of English history are so imperfectly

4. In his article "Ceremony and History: The Problem of Symbol from *Richard II* to *Henry V*," which appears in *Pacific Coast Studies in Shakespeare*, ed. Waldo F. McNeir and Thelma N. Greenfield (Eugene, Ore., 1966), Eric La Guardia finds language turning away from poetry in *Henry V* and "into policy, certainly a result in part of a Falstaffian education in expediency, but non-Falstaffian in the King's narrow and arid use of verbal forms" (pp. 82–83). Elsewhere La Guardia says that the tetralogy is a "drama of the decline of poetical man and the rise of rhetorical man [that] is also the drama of the collectivisation of language" (p. 86).

approached. Truth and value do not reside in theatrical presentation, any more than perfect circularity resides in a particular representation of a circle. *Henry V* acts upon the imagination of its audiences in such a way as to reach toward historical truths which it is, in itself, incapable of compassing.

As usual, Shakespeare is ahead of us. Thus he reminds us in his Epilogue that what King Harry achieved was soon lost, which suggests—if the kinship between king and dramatist holds true—that Shakespeare's own dramatic achievements are fugitive, that in deploying his artistic means toward shaping this nationalistic play he has found only a stop-gap solution to theatrical enigmas of enduring complexity. But that, after all, is the fate of means. Having no instrinsic value, they serve the needs of the occasion and then, as occasions change, fall from fashion. Rhetoric is cursed with built-in obsolescence; it inspires and, having attained its end, dissolves with all the finality of a Shakespearean performance. It may be revived, like *Henry V* itself, whenever war is again in favor and the hackles of the populace need raising. Another Harry, in the person of a Maurice Evans, for instance, may tour the battlefields of another war, crying "Once more unto the breach, dear friends, once more!" For the moment, in *Henry V*, Shakespeare may settle uneasily for that kind of verbal efficacy. But finding truth and meaning through one's art is a far cry from finding them *in* one's art. So the word serves its turn as rhetoric in *Henry V*, and epic drama serves its turn as stimulus of the patriotic imagination, and for a time the English, both in Harry's kingdom and in Shakespeare's theater, are bound in brotherhood. "Small time," the Chorus says, "but in that small most greatly lived / This star of England" (Epilogue). The small time of history has become even smaller on Shakespeare's stage. History is linear and unrepeatable, except in drama, and now that Shakespeare has freed his own drama from the eddying of 2 *Henry IV* it too has become linear and unrepeatable. The dramatic succession moves on, and we have not long to wait before *Hamlet* addresses itself by indirections to those familiar unresolved issues of theatrical illusion and poisoned speech.

Appendix:

ELIZABETHAN NAMING

When Prince Hal, fresh from bloodless triumphs at Gadshill, prepares to move against even greater rebels, he rallies his alehouse legions with phrases out of Hotspur's rhetoric:

> The land is burning; Percy stands on high;
> And either we or they must lower lie.

An aroused Falstaff trumpets his response—"Rare words! Brave world!"—and then, as the departing Hal passes beyond earshot, adds: "Hostess, my breakfast, come! / O, I could wish this tavern were my drum!" (1 *Hen. IV*, 3.3.227–230). Here as elsewhere—more famously of course in his speech on honor—Falstaff is self-protectively dubious about the virtue of "rare" words in the brave world, for if such words are, in one sense of "rare," extraordinary and splendid, they are also, in another sense, insubstantial and airy. And so at Shrewsbury Field, when the wild Douglas's sword is carving the air at his own most substantial backside, Falstaff wisely does not pause to orate.

Harry Hotspur, on the other hand, is more credulous about the relation of rare words to the brave world. It is true that "mincing poetry" sets his teeth on edge (3.1.129ff.) and that Glendower's verbal powers do not impress him:

Appendix

Glendower: I can call spirits from the vasty deep.
Hotspur: Why, so can I, or so can any man;
           But will they come when you do call for
           them?

(3.1.53–55)

Poetic and magical words are simply not part of Hotspur's vocabulary. Change the names, however, situate words like "truth," "esperance," or "honor" within the vasty deep, and Harry will not merely call them but

dive into the bottom of the deep
Where fathom line could never touch the ground
And pluck up drowned Honour by the locks.

(1.2.203–205)

Most Elizabethans were not prepared to go quite so far, certainly not nearly so deep, as Hotspur in their commitments to language, and yet on the whole they felt that words were in close covenant with the world.[1]

1. Information about Elizabethan attitudes toward language is not easily come by, although there are many learned discussions of the language itself—its orthographic vagaries, confiscations of foreign words, search for eloquence and elegance, and so on. Molly Mahood has a perceptive summary of contemporary views in *Shakespeare's Wordplay* (London, 1957), pp. 169–175; Walter Ong writes illuminatingly about the impact of print on the oral-aural aspects of Elizabethan England in *The Presence of the Word* (New Haven and London, 1967), especially pp. 192–287; and Gerald L. Bruns has an excellent chapter on the "foregrounding" or substantializing of language in rhetoric and grammar from the Greeks through the Renaissance, in *Modern Poetry and the Idea of Language* (New Haven and London, 1974), pp. 11–41. The most thorough treatment of Elizabethan language is Richard Foster Jones's *The Triumph of the English Language* (Stanford, 1953). See also his *Ancients and Moderns* (St. Louis, 1961; 2nd ed., Berkeley and

Given their view of the origin of language, it could hardly have been otherwise. For the dominant assumption of the time—and indeed until 1772 when Herder put the notion to rest[2]—was that human speech is, at least vestigially, a divine institution. "The first author of Speech," said Thomas Hobbes, echoing the Elizabethan belief, "was *God* himself, that instructed *Adam* how to name such creatures as he presented to his sight" *(Leviathan*, I, ch. 4). Not only did God invest Adam with speech but, on the authority of Saint John, "In the beginning was the Word, and the Word was with God, and the Word was God." So close was the bond between God and the Word that Creation was accomplished not by a divine willing, imagining, or material constructing; instead, God *spoke* the world into being—"And God said, Let there be. . . ."[3]

Los Angeles, 1965) and his fine article on "Science and Language in England of the Mid-Seventeenth Century," *Journal of English and Germanic Philology* 31 (1932): 315–331.

2. In his essay *Concerning the Origin of Language*, Johann Gottfried von Herder repudiated Johann P. Sussmilch's contention that language is an outright gift to man from God. If that were so, Herder argued, language would surely have been more logical than it is. Though man's impulse to speak may have been from God, he fashioned language on his own.

3. In many cosmogonic myths, words are the midwives of divine creativity. Sometimes they are even the instruments by which the god creates himself. The Egyptian god Neberdjer existed in name only until, as Sir E. A. Wallis Budge says, "the god took counsel with his heart, and possessing magical power (heka), he uttered his own name as a spell or word of power, and he straightway came into being under the form of the god Khepera, and began the work of creation" (*Amulets and Talismans* [New York,

Appendix

A similar union of words and things was thought to exist in the *lingua Adamica* or *lingua humana,* as it was variously called—the natural language of Eden that issued spontaneously from Adam's lips when God paraded the creatures before him "to see what he would call them" (*Genesis,* 2:19).[4] If God's speech was creative, Adam's was at least correlative, though just what language Adam spoke was subject to considerable dispute. Jacob Boehme claimed it was the "sensual

---

1961], p. 7). The Egyptian sun-god Rā is said to have employed the same method of manifesting himself, and his colleague Thoth, the Egyptian word-god, brought all material things into being through his utterances.

4. Adam's divinely inspired sense of language must have seemed to sixteenth-century Platonists a spectacular instance of God's generosity and a confirmation of innate knowledge. The notion that language exists in man before he learns to speak, as Merleau-Ponty claims, appeared also in the seventeenth century, beginning with Descartes, the Port-Royal grammarians, Cordemoy, and culminating with Humbolt in the nineteenth century. Common to this group of "Cartesian linguists"—see Noam Chomsky, *Cartesian Linguistics* (New York, 1966), pp. 59–73—is the belief that language, if not innately known to man, is nevertheless implicit in the structure of the human mind. Chomsky takes a similar position today: "We cannot claim that every child is born with a perfect knowledge of English. On the other hand, there is no reason why we should not suppose that the child is born with a perfect knowledge of universal grammar, that is, with a fixed schematism that he uses . . . in acquiring language" ("Linguistics and Philosophy" in *Language and Philosophy,* ed. Sidney Hook [New York, 1969], p. 88). Presumably, the generative grammar of transformational linguistics was built into Adam's mind before the animals came seeking their names, just as Eve was immanent in his rib even before that first fatal act of feminine liberation.

speech" of nature herself, which enabled souls to address one another without the meddlesome mediation of words—an early spiritual version, presumably, of what linguists sometimes call "kinesics."[5] On the other hand, the traditional Christian view, set forth in some detail by Augustine in *The City of God* (bk. 16, ch. 11) and repeated throughout the sixteenth and seventeenth centuries, favored Hebrew, which was thought to be so innate to the human mind that children reared in isolation would come to speak it naturally. (This assumption was put to the test by James IV of Scotland, who supposedly declared upon examining them afterwards that the children "spak very guid Ebrew."[6]) Other verbal candidates for the *lingua humana* were

5. Jacob Boehme, *Mysterium Magnum*, ch. 35, secs. 59–60; cited by Norman O. Brown, *Life Against Death* (Middletown, Conn., 1959), p. 72. Boehme, apparently, first coined the term *lingua Adamica*.

6. This experiment by James IV is similar to one reported by Herodotus in which the Egyptian king Psammetichus, anxious to determine whether the Egyptians or the Phrygians were the most ancient people, handed two children over to herdsmen (some said to women whose tongues had been cut out) to raise in isolation. Their first word after the babbling stage was "Becos," which turned out to be the Phrygian word for bread, so the unhappy Egyptians were obliged to concede the greater antiquity of the Phrygians (see *The History of Herodotus*, trans. George Rawlinson, [New York, 1928], pp. 81–82). My learned friend Max Yeh claims—on the authority of his fading recollection of a passing remark during a lecture given by a history professor when he was a freshman—that Frederick Barbarossa conducted a similar experiment, isolating two children on an island to see if their first words would be Hebrew. As Professor Yeh recalls, however, they spoke no Hebrew —perhaps Phrygian.

Scythian, Danish, even Celtic. But most flattering to
the English was the view of the Flemish physician
Joannes Goropius Becanus, who proclaimed in 1580
that the original speech of both Adam and the Old
Testament had been German—at least until God, fear-
ful lest man grow overproud with the Germanic clarity
of sacred truths, caused the Old Testament to be translated into the obscurities of Hebrew.[7] The case for German, with a special Scandinavian bias, was reinforced
by a seventeenth-century Swedish philologist, Andreas
Kemke, who argued that in the garden of Eden God
spoke Swedish, Adam Danish, and the serpent French
—which does have the ring of truth to it.

Whatever the chosen speech was, Adam's first
words were not merely arbitrary labels or differentiat-
ing tags but the true, the real names. As our mental
images correspond to the things they reflect "out there,"
said Athanasius Kircher in *Turris Babel* (1679), so
Adam's words corresponded exactly to the objects they
represented. And just as man's sense impressions are
the same everywhere and at all times, so the *lingua
humana* as a whole mirrored reality perfectly. Or, as
Max Picard puts it, "When words and things were
still a unity, when words did not describe things but
were things, and things named themselves simply by
existing, there was no problem of language. Words
were absorbed in things and things in words, each was
cherished by the other."[8] So the situation remained,

7. R. F. Jones discusses Goropius's curious theory and
its influence in England in *The Triumph of the English Language* (see note 1 above), pp. 215–218.

8. Max Picard, *Man and Language* (Chicago, 1963), p.
18. For information about the remarkable Athanasius Kir-

words binding man and nature into one community, until Adam's vocabulary expanded to include the terms *good* and *evil,* after which God added *nakedness, exile, work,* and *death.* Estranged now from God and nature, men remained bound at least to one another by virtue of their common, if fallen, language, which at Babel brought them together in a community of unwise aspiration symbolized by the raising of a tower and the forging of a name (*Genesis,* 11:4). But in what Bacon called the "second curse," man's medium of solidarity became God's instrument of division as He shivered the language into a thousand dialects and scattered man over the earth. By Shakespeare's time, though Cabbalists and linguists still dreamed of recovering the lost *lingua Adamica,* not all the king's antiquarians could put the Humpty-Dumpty of Edenic speech together again.[9]

---

cher, who was Professor of Oriental Languages at the Roman College of the Jesuits, see D. C. Allen, *The Legend of Noah* (Urbana, Ill., 1949); and for an account of Kircher's linguistic views, especially as regards an ideal universal language, see Paul Cornelius, *Languages in Seventeenth and Early Eighteenth Century Imaginary Voyages* (Geneva, 1965), esp. pp. 5–23.

9. Searching for the *lingua Adamica,* however, was less popular among late sixteenth-century antiquarians and linguists in England than restoring dignity and value to the German language, from which English was now seen to derive by way of Saxon. That is, once the legendary notions about England's Trojan origins came into doubt and a Teutonic derivation was assumed, it then became necessary to stop lamenting and begin dignifying the Anglo-Saxon tongue. Richard Verstegan and William Camden—whose *A Restitution of Decayed Intelligence* and *Remains of a Greater Work, Concerning Britain* both appeared in 1605

Appendix

The biblical account of the rise and fall of Edenic speech roughly conforms to the process of division and abstraction hypothesized in prehistoric language by students of symbolism hardy enough to venture into that dark backward and abysm of time.[10] Adam's bestowal of a name on each animal—the primitive creation of symbol—was surely the most revolutionary act in the history of human consciousness, something anal-

---

—took the lead in proclaiming the virtues of the Saxons, noblest and most well-spoken of Teutonic peoples. With the noteworthy exception of Samuel Daniel, most early Elizabethans had condemned the Goths as a general source of barbarism in language and learning; but toward the end of the sixteenth and up to the middle of the seventeenth century, English hospitality to things Germanic, especially in language, flourished. As R. F. Jones notes, "A lectureship in [Anglo-Saxon] was established at Cambridge [in 1623], poems were written in [Anglo-Saxon], a lexicon of it was compiled, and it takes its place beside Latin, Greek, and Hebrew, the learned languages" (*The Triumph of the English Language*, pp. 232–233). The Germanic antiquity of English now became a mark of its native excellence. And if few believed with Goropius and Ortelius that German was itself the language of Adam and Eve, many believed that because it was the language of an unconquered people (in parts of Germany at any rate) it had been less affected by the confusion of tongues wrought at Babel and through conquest.

10. For instance, Otto Jesperson, *Language: Its Nature, Development, and Origin* (New York, 1922); Richard A. Wilson, *The Miraculous Birth of Language* (London, 1937); Suzanne Langer, *Philosophy in a New Key* (Cambridge, Mass., 1942); Ernst Cassirer, *Language and Myth* (New York, 1946); Owen Barfield, *Saving the Appearances* (London, 1948); A. S. Diamond, *The History and Origin of Language* (London, 1959); and Morris Swadesh, *The Origin and Diversification of Languages* (London, 1972).

ogous on a large scale to Helen Keller's discovery that water had a name. By giving him a verbal grip on individual features of experience—thus endowing him with memory and hence ultimately with a personal history—the name liberated man from the bondage of time and vaulted him eventually into the domain of thought. In a world of linguo-mythic unity of the sort postulated by Ernst Cassirer and others,[11] word and thing, symbol and symbolized, human subject and natural object are one. Nature hears and understands man's speech, and in so doing she renders herself vulnerable to his word magic.

Speech of this sort, in which words participate in things, is usually held to be nominalistic, a language devoted to particulars, like that of the Bakairi of Central Brazil which has names for each type of parrot and palm tree but no names to denote the generic "parrot" or "palm."[12] When participative speech breaks

---

11. On the familiar topic of the primitive solidarity of life, see Lucien Lévy-Bruhl, *How Natives Think* (London, 1926); Bronislaw Malinowski, *Crime and Custom in Savage Society* (New York, 1926); Carl J. Jung's "Archaic Man" in *Modern Man in Search of a Soul* (1933); and Erich Kahler, *Man the Measure* (New York, 1943), pp. 24–49. On the verbal consequences of such solidarity, see Sir James G. Frazer's chapter "Tabooed Words" in the abridged version of *The Golden Bough* (New York, 1958), pp. 284–304; Suzanne Langer's chapter on "Language" in *Philosophy in a New Key* (see note 10 above); and Ernst Cassirer's *Language and Myth* (see note 10 above) and *An Essay on Man* (New Haven, 1944).

12. This primitive inability to see the forest for the trees seems literally the case with Tasmanian aborigines, who have names for each kind of gum tree and wattle tree but no name for "tree" itself. The notion that man's earliest

down and the discreteness of words and things becomes apparent, man discovers that in what he had thought to be his dialogue with nature he was merely talking to himself. If nature had failed to respond to his magical words it was not that his timing was wrong or nature hostile; she simply did not speak his language. Following from this unpleasant discovery are man's estrangement from nature, an enduring sense of forlornness, and the dubious consolations of civilization.

This gloomy rendering of man's early ventures among speech is modeled, as it was in Elizabethan times, upon the biblical "fall." Modern linguists, however, see the same process through melioristic spectacles. For them the breakdown of the union of word and thing becomes the liberation of the word from the

---

speech dwelt on particulars is a reversal of the nineteenth-century belief—expressed most popularly by Max Müller in his *Lectures on the Science of Language* (1861–1864)—that the earliest utterances were highly abstract "root" terms like *shine* or *cut*, which were then combined or elaborated as metaphors. But as Otto Jesperson argued in *Language: Its Nature, Development, and Origin* (London, 1922), as we move back toward the origins of speech, words get longer, not shorter, so that very early languages deal not in freely combinable roots but in holophrastic utterances—long inseparable conglomerations of sound referring to highly specific instances. As Walter Ong observes, "Even a language developed as far as classical Latin regularly uses forms such as *cogitavisset*, which would break down in an 'older' or later-stage language such as modern English into separate elements, 'he would have thought' " (*The Presence of the Word* (see note 1 above), p. 152; see also Owen Barfield, *Saving the Appearances* (see note 10 above), pp. 116–125).

thing. Imbruted in matter until now, the soul of symbolicity is freed for a generalizing ascent, a transcending movement analogous to Adam's "graduation" from a concrete naming of creatures to a consciousness of such verbal universals as good and evil. Viewed from this perspective of progress, his being cast out of the natural world by means of language is simply the price man had to pay for the creation of subject and object, self and nature, neither of which fully existed until they were parted by words. But whether conceived of as a fall from grace and wholeness or as a disburdening of rude matter, it is clear that in the long run of meaning the Word has become quite disengaged from the concrete stuff of the world's body.

These issues may seem disengaged from the concrete stuff of Shakespeare's four history plays too; and yet it is just this movement—this "fall' from an Eden of ontological symbolism into a desert of arbitrary signs—that these plays reflect. Or, rather, discover— for the divorce of language from reality is only nascent at the time of their writing. From his own deep engagement with language Shakespeare evidently sensed a subliminal drift of culture that was not to become publicly manifest until the science and philosophy of the seventeenth century—sensed and articulated it, not in forward-looking treatises like *The Advancement of Learning,* but, with assays of backward bias, in plays about English "history." These plays are not, therefore, mimetic reflections of the linguistic revolution I am describing in this appendix, for the revolution was only potentially emergent—discoverable but not yet imitable.

Having in the foregoing chapters sought to show

how the cultural issues are immanent in *The Henriad,* I shall try here to suggest how those issues achieved discursive definition in the sixteenth and seventeenth centuries. The following section focuses primarily on the prominence of verbal realism in and before Shakespeare's time—on a kind of language that can be variously called ontological, participative, sacramental, magical—and the third section stresses the breakdown of this kind of language.

*

The fact that Elizabethans cherished the word as word is owing in large part to the sacralizing of speech not only in the Bible but in Christianity as well. When man fell, his language fell too: and when he partially rose up again due to the ministrations of Christ the Logos, his language recaptured something of its former grace also. A passage from Augustine's sermons on the Psalms suggests the pivotal role of the word as mediator between God, nature, and man in the long dialogue of spiritual history:

> All other things may be expressed in some way; He alone is ineffable, Who spoke, and all things were made. He spoke, and we were made; but we are unable to speak to Him. His Word, by Whom we were spoken, is His Son. He was made weak, so that He might be spoken by us, despite our weakness.[13]

As Marcia Colish observes: "For Augustine, then, God creates the world and man through His Word, and He

13. *Ennaratio in Psalmum,* 99: 6, *Corpus Christianotum,*

takes on humanity in the Word made flesh so that human words may take on Divinity, thereby bringing man and the world back to God."[14] Christ the Word empowers human speech, now redeemed, to continue the work of the Incarnation; Christian eloquence bears God's Word to mankind.

In *De Oratore* Cicero assigns to language a similar, if more secular function in elevating mankind:

> To come, however, at length to the highest achievements of eloquence, what other power could have been strong enough either to gather scattered humanity into one place, or to lead it out of its brutish existence in the wilderness up to our present condition of civilization as men and as citizens, or, after the establishment of social communities, to give shape to laws, tribunals, and civic rights.[15]

39: 1397; cited by Marcia Colish, *The Mirror of Language* (New Haven and London, 1968), p. 35.

14. *Ibid.*

15. Cicero, *De Oratore*, 2 vols., trans. E. W. Sutton, completed by H. Rackham (Cambridge, Mass. and London, 1959), 1:8:33. To account for the civilizing of man, Elizabethans usually drew on classical myths featuring the powers of poetic language, as William Webbe did in his *A Discourse of English Poetrie* (see G. Gregory Smith's *Elizabethan Critical Essays* [London, 1904], 1:234) when he said "the best wryters agree that it was *Orpheus*, who by the sweete gyft of his heavenly poetry withdrew men from raungyng uncertainly and wandring brutishly about, and made them gather together and keepe company, make houses, and keep fellowshippe together, who therefore is reported (as *Horace* sayth) to asswage the fiercenesse of Tygers and moove the harde Flynts. After him was *Amphion*, who was the first that caused Cities to bee builded,

And in his *Art of Rhetoric* (1560) Thomas Wilson appears to combine these Christian and pagan rhetorical notions in a theory of man's Fall and Redemption that centers in his loss and gradual reacquisition of the divine gift of eloquence.[16] After man had fallen, Wilson says, "long it was ere man knewe himselfe being destitute of Gods grace, so that all thinges waxed savage, the earth untilled, societie neglected, Gods will not known, man against man, one against an other, and all against order." Though man seemed beyond amendment in this brutish state, God mercifully "gave his appointed Ministers knowledge both to see the natures of men, and also granted them the gift of utteraunce, that they might with ease win folke at their will, and frame them by reason to all good order." As Wilson warms to his theme it appears that the tightrope of eloquence is all that prevents man from plunging again into bestial abysses. And for some special few possessed of erected wit and singing phrases, an almost Pico-like escalation toward heavenly forms appears possible: "For he that is among the reasonable of all most reasonable, and among the wittie, of all most wittie, and among the eloquent, of all most eloquent: him thinke I amonge all men, not onely to be taken for a singuler man, but rather to be coumpted for halfe a God." If God's words once spoke man into existence in His likeness—this, the first mimetic work of art: "Let us make man in our image, after our likeness (*Genesis,*

---

and men therein to live decently and orderly according to lawe and right."

16. Thomas Wilson, *Arte of Rhetorique,* rev. ed., 1560 (ed. G. H. Mair, Oxford, 1909); the following quotations are from Wilson's preface.

1:26)—man's own redeemed words can at least halfway restore that lost likeness. Wilson's sentiments are
akin to those of Scaliger on poetry—"But the poet
makes another nature and other outcomes of men's
acts, and finally in the same way makes himself another
God, as it were" (*Poetices Libri Septem*, 1561, 1, 1, 3)
—and of Sidney, who sees the poet reasserting his own
divine nature in the act of delivering golden worlds in
verse (*Defense of Poesie*, 2, 9–11).

The gap between divine and human nature is
bridged when God unites the two in the Word made
flesh—an ethereal meaning incorporated into an earthly body. This concept of the incarnate Word appears
in secular forms as well, as when Castiglione's Count
says that "to separate thoughts from words is to separate soul from body: in neither case can it be done
without destruction," or when Ben Jonson says "In all
speech, words and sense are as the body and the soule.
The sense is as the life and soul of Language, without
which all words are dead."[17] A similar conception appears in a passage in *Musophilus* where Samuel Daniel
speaks of the sustaining "body" of words in which the
authorial spirit may live:

> For these lines are the veins, the arteries,
> And undecaying life-strings of those hearts
> That still shall pant, and still shall exercise
> The motion, spirit and nature both imparts;
> And shall with those alive so sympathize
> As nourished with their powers, enjoy their parts.[18]

17. Baldesar Castiglione, *The Book of the Courtier*, trans.
Charles S. Singleton (New York, 1959), p. 54. Ben Jonson,
Timber, or Discoveries in *English Literary Criticism: The
Renaissance*, ed. O. B. Hardison (New York, 1963), p. 278.

18. Samuel Daniel, "Musophilus," in *Tudor Poetry and*

As the rhetoricians hold, the perfect union of a semantic soul in a verbal body gives rise to eloquence, the end of fine speaking; and a down-to-earth educator like Roger Ascham can give the incarnation metaphor a homely turn by arguing that "good and choice meates be no more requisite for helthie bodies than proper and apte wordes be for good matters, and also plaine and sensible utterance for the best and depest reasons: in which two pointes standeth perfite eloquence, one of the fairest and rarest giftes that God doth geve man."[19]

For the sixteenth-century Christian, religious faith and verbal faith coalesce, most noticeably in prayer and ritual. In prayer the spoken word is endowed by faith with magical powers. One thinks for instance of the incremental virtue imputed to the sheer substance of sound in repetitive prayer—the "worth" of so many Hail Marys, so many paternosters, and so on—or simply of the fact of prayer itself, that God should be addressed by voiced entreaties instead of, say, propitiatory sacrifice.[20] The sovereignty of the word is further emphasized when prayer draws on the binding force of sacred names. "In the name of God" and "In the name of Christ" are as indispensable as "Open sesame" in unlocking the gates of spiritual treasure. And if, like

---

Prose, ed. J. W. Hebel and H. H. Hudson (New York, 1953), p. 270.

19. Roger Ascham, *The Scholemaster,* in Smith's *Elizabethan Critical Essays,* (see note 15 above) 1:6.

20. "Voiced" entreaties because whereas God may have, as it were, written to man in the Bible, man speaks to but does not write to God in return—presumably because writing implies the absence of the addressee, which would conflict with the omnipresence of God, Who must be within hearing even of whispered devotions.

Doctor Faustus, one knows the proper black magical arts, the power of divine names can be called on diabolically:

> Within this circle is Jehovah's name
> Forward and backward anagrammatized,
> The abbreviated names of holy saints. . . .

Or, in more orthodox ceremonies, there are the magical powers of the priest during Communion, whose voicing of the words "This is my body, this is my blood" can, if he is Catholic, transubstantiate all but the accidental properties of the bread and wine or, if he is Protestant, remove the veil of matter from them and disclose the divine presence housed within.

The written word, too, especially in biblical form, exercised an influence on Elizabethan conceptions of language that can hardly be overrated. I mean not merely the prominence given the word in the Bible— its "In the beginning was the Word" or its association of Christ with Logos—nor the immense shaping of the English sensibility by the biblical translations of Wyclif, Tyndale, Coverdale, and others up to the King James version, but rather the very bookishness of the Bible. "It was through Christianity," Ernst Curtius has said, "that the book received its highest consecration. Christianity was a religion of the Holy Book. Christ is the only god whom antique art represents with a book-scroll."[21] The reverence accorded the Holy Book inevitably rubbed off on ordinary books and words as well, so that verbal expression in general would seem

---

21. Ernst Robert Curtius, *European Literature and the Latin Middle Ages*, trans. W. R. Trask (London, 1953), p. 310.

a natural vehicle of truth, as it would not have done had Christian religion centered, say, in ritual, like Dionysiac or Orphic cults. Indeed, the medieval acceptance of the Holy Bible prepares the way in some degree for the Renaissance acceptance of the classical books. The Renaissance "new learning" takes the classical "word" on a kind of religious faith, believing that the antique word in its various forms—as history, astronomy, metaphysics, philosophy, literature, law, medicine—truly reflects the structure of reality. Thus with Puritans single-mindedly intent on their Bibles and humanists poring over Cicero and Virgil, Caliban's "possess his books, for without them / He's but a sot, as I am" might well sum up the cultural fact that for Elizabethans nearly the whole of civilized human experience came under the aegis of language.

Whatever the causes, Elizabethans did endow words with sovereignty and intrinsic worth. Only a cherishing of language in and for itself could induce a Henry Peacham to catalogue, define, and copiously exemplify 191 types of figure in *The Garden of Eloquence* (1577) or could arouse the gustatory savor of Thomas Wilson's "Yea, words that fill the mouth and have a sound with them, set forth a matter very well. And sometimes words twice spoken, make the matter appear greater."[22] Only a rooted conviction of the almost physical efficacy of speech could power the verbal cannonades of Greene, Harvey, Nashe, Lyly, Marston, and Jonson as they assault one another with what Puttenham calls "fleering frumps," "dry mocks," and "broad flouts." The rancor of the wounded testifies to

22. Thomas Wilson, *Arte of Rhetorique* (see note 16 above) p. 114.

the fact that in these satiric wars the verbal weaponry is more than metaphorically murderous. And one is struck by the fact too that late Elizabethan satire is conducted not only in words but over words—that even more than usual in satire the disputes center in language and poetry instead of politics, religion, or social conduct. Nothing rouses Nashe to fury like a list of Gabriel Harvey's latest inkhornisms—some of the "new ingendred fome" on the English language which he says Harvey has "scummed off"—unless it is a suggestion that Nashe's own prose style is secondhand.[23]

The popularity of name-calling among Elizabethans is appropriate, since for them names, rather than verbs, adjectives, or prepositions, were the essence of language. And names were not merely conventional symbols but the shadows or images of things. Scientist-occultists like Paracelsus, who claimed that in nature "everything that is within can be known by what is without," could still regard names as the outward manifestations of inner realities, so that "each being should be given the name that belongs to its essence."[24]

23. See the extracts from Nashe's *Strange Newes, or Foure Letters Confuted* (1592) in Smith's *Elizabethan Critical Essays*, 1:242. Most of the major salvos of the Greene-Harvey-Nashe engagement are recorded by Smith.

24. Paracelsus, "Man and Words" in *Selected Writings* (London, 1951), pp. 194–212. Similar views held by such occultists as Agrippa, the Paduan physician Jerome Cardan, and Dr. John Dee derived in part from the Neoplatonic assumption of the Florentine Academy that between angels and devils are multitudes of unbodied spirits to which man is akin. This and the belief that nature is invested with hidden virtues transmitted "to all physical objects by the stars from the intellectual world, which in turn emanated from God, [tended] to blur the difference between matter and

On this view language becomes a reliable index to nature—even, like color and form, a constituent of nature—so that the concept of the "book" of nature takes on a literal significance. Paracelsus's notion of named essences in nature is akin to the primitive belief that a man's name is not merely a distinguishing sign but the true sum of his being, a belief that gained some biblical support from Christ's punning on "Peter" as the rocklike foundation of his Church. In any event, if names do reflect inner being, then he who controls names controls things as well. To call spirits from the vasty deep or from ethereal regions, or to exorcize them from the soul, names are indispensable. Robert Elliott has brilliantly demonstrated how word-magic, based on a substantive identity of name and thing, gradually passes through magical satire and ridicule and thence to satire as literary art, much as ritual gives rise to drama.[25]

---

spirit" ("God and Expansion in Elizabethan England: John Dee, 1527–1583," by Walter I. Trattner, *Journal of the History of Ideas* 25 [1964]: 22). Thus magic, with considerable emphasis upon verbal charms and invocations, becomes possible. For a shrewd discussion of magic, neo-platonism, and empiricism, see C. S. Lewis, *English Literature in the Sixteenth Century* (Oxford, 1954), pp. 1–14.

25. Robert C. Elliott, *The Power of Satire* (Princeton, 1960). The Tetragrammaton and other unpronounceable or secret names for gods issued from the belief in the identity of name and thing. Such names were designed to prevent men from making claims on the god or usurping his powers, as Isis usurped some of Rā's powers on learning his true name (see Frazer's account in the abridged *Golden Bough* [note 11 above], pp. 302–305). According to Mario Pei, "in medieval Hebrew Cabalistic lore, *ba'al šēm* ('master of the name') was one who knew the secret vowels of

If names could kill by magic, and sorely wound by satire, they could also give life. Baptism, either of the newborn or of priests and nuns following their novitiates, imparted new life and a cleansed identity. A woman's adoption of her husband's name in marriage also symbolized a transformation of being. The marital name in itself may not have guaranteed masculine property rights or conjured up feminine "honesty" —even for Elizabethans word-magic had its limits, as the ubiquitous puns on cuckoldry imply—but even so, the sharing of family name was probably felt to entail a sharing of identity that would seem curious today. Titles of honor too gave new life. In fact, the Renaissance king "created" men ("creation" was the official term for it) by conferring knighthood upon them, and in 1611 King James created a whole new order of men by instituting the baronetage. Even to a verbal skeptic like Bolingbroke the noble name has the substantiality of inherited property, so that on his return from exile in France he can reply to Berkeley's "My Lord of Hereford, my message is to you" with—

> My lord, my answer is—to Lancaster.
> And I am come to seek that name in England,
> And I must find that title in your tongue
> Before I make reply to aught you say.
> <div align="right">(<i>Rich. II</i>, 2.3.69–79)</div>

This is not the place to launch into a full-scale cataloguing of Elizabethan verbal realism. The point is simply that at this time language was on the whole

---

the word 'Jehovah,' which knowledge gave him enormous magical powers" (*The Story of Language*, rev. ed. [Philadelphia and New York, 1965], p. 253).

an object of belief—not merely a system of empty signs directing its users to a world of independent things but, insofar as this is possible in nonprimitive and nonpoetic language, a system of "rare words," as Falstaff says, in which the "brave world" is implicit. The word both is and does. It has substantive being not only in itself but insofar as it participates in the things it symbolizes, and it is empowered by virtue of this participation to act upon and in the world of things. Thus words can become objects of veneration in themselves. "The age believed wholeheartedly in the literary value of its language," R. F. Jones has said. "It was not viewed merely as a medium of expression for literary conceptions; its refinement furnished an objective for literature, became, in fact, an important goal of literary activity. To serve the mother tongue was proposed as one motive in writing as early as Spenser and as late as Milton."[26]

*

Adam was his own most singular self, and in the beginning, it is said, words followed suit, producing for instance holophrastic utterances, long conglomerations of sound referring to precise, individual cases, like the Fuegan *mamihlapinatapai*, which means, of course, "that situation in which two people are looking at one

26. Jones, *The Triumph of the English Language* (see note 1 above), p. 212. This veneration of English is in distinct contrast to the view held during the first three-quarters of the sixteenth century when the language was regarded as rude, coarse, barbaric, but especially uneloquent, fit only (in comparison to Latin) to instruct the uneducated.

another, each hoping the other will do something they both desire but are unwilling to undertake." From such local and concrete expressions as this, the course of verbal meaning advances steadily toward the universal and abstract, from "Adam," as it were, to "atomic." In these latter days holophrases are hard to come by amid statistical data, the symbolic notations of chemistry and physics, and the formalized languages of logicians. From speech oriented to a radical "thisness" we pass not only to deserts of verbal abstraction but even out beyond speech itself. This long movement from holophrase to statistic is reflected in brief form at certain points in history—in Greece, for instance, when philosophy supplanted Homer in the Greek *paideia*, when the concrete namings of the mythopoeic imagination faded into the abstract essences of Socratic-Platonic reason. A similar development took place in Shakespeare's time when the participative language I have been describing began to lose its purchase on reality and give way to empirical science. Since trying to account for this in proper detail would go a long way toward making a man look sad, let me miniaturize the matter in terms of the Book of Nature.

That nature was regarded as a "book" is owing primarily to Christianity, the religion of the Book. In classical sign theory, words had been only one of many species of sign; but for Augustine, words became the essence of signification. If God originally spoke the world into being, then all creation is His "expression" —a complex symbolic utterance that requires skilled interpretation. Ernst Curtius has traced the history of the Christian Book of Nature *topos* from its origin in

pulpit metaphor, through medieval speculative thought,
and into common usage.[27] Before receiving its Christian
imprimatur, however, the book of nature came out in
a pagan edition of sorts. When Democritus cast about
for a name for the elements of air, earth, fire, and water,
he hit finally upon *stoikheion* ($\sigma\tau o\iota\chi\epsilon\hat{\iota}o\nu$), which meant
"a speech sound" or, today, a "phone"—not strictly a
letter (*grammaton*) though occasionally it meant that
too. Anyhow, with everything made up of these four
voiced elements, the entire world becomes in Democritus's metaphor a verbal structure—an oration or
book—and each of its parts, presumably, a distinct
word. Later on, to identify the four humors which constituted the mind and body of man, Galen took a page,
or at least a word, from Democritus, translating
stoikheion into its Latin equivalent, *elementum*—"a
letter of the alphabet."[28] With both his body and tem-
perament determined by a singular fusion of Demo-
critian and Galenic "elements," man becomes not only
a speaking animal but a spoken one, a verbal composition. In light of this, Antony's words over the dead
Brutus are most apt:

27. Ernst Curtius, *European Literature and the Latin
Middle Ages*, trans. Willard R. Trask (New York, 1953),
pp. 319–326.

28. Leo Spitzer, *Classical and Christian Ideas of World
Harmony* (Baltimore, 1963), p. 65. Even the anti-Galenist
Paracelsus, whose bodily "elements" were not the humors
but the chemicals mercury, salt, and sulphur, believed none-
theless in a complete correspondence between man and nature. As Marjorie Nicholson says, "[For Paracelsus] man
was the elements; he was minerals and metals; he was
fruit and trees, vegetables and flowers. He was also winds
and storms and tempests" (*The Breaking of the Circle*, rev.
ed. [New York, 1960], p. 23).

Elizabethan Naming

His life was gentle, and the elements
So mixed in him that Nature might stand up
And say to all the world, "This was a man!"
(*Caesar*, 5.5.73–75)

Brutus is united with Nature by the "elements"
of which both are composed, the "letters" that eloquently combine to make Brutus not only a microcosm
but a microword. Thus if Nature declines to stand and
speak *about* the dead Brutus, it is because she has already said her piece *in* the living Brutus. He has been
one of her finer articulations.

The Book of Nature metaphor is still alive, at
least in literary quarters, during the nineteenth century,
and as far into the twentieth as Wallace Stevens, for
whom it becomes versified as "the essential poem at
the centre of things" (in "A Primitive Like an Orb"),
or Galway Kinnell, for whom it becomes an uninter-
preted voicing of itself:

> the leaf
> shaped tongue
> of the new born and the dying
> quivers, and no one interprets it.
> ("The Poem")

Outside the pages of poets, however, the figure of Nature's book or voice has fared less well. It is not that
"no one interprets it" but that Nature's language has
turned so abstruse that few can make it out, and even
they move their lips.

Until the seventeenth century no one doubted that
the Book of Nature was intelligible to man. Profound,
to be sure, and symbolic, and perhaps even veiled—as
befitted a God Who, after the Fall, could reveal Him-

Appendix

self only in a dark conceit—but nevertheless intelligible. The beginnings of a different attitude toward Nature's language take perceptible shape in Francis Bacon. Bacon can speak of the Book of Nature in perfectly conventional terms, as in his introduction to the "Nature and Experimental History," Part III of the *Magna Instauratio*:

> we must exhort men again and again . . . to approach with humility and veneration to unroll the volume of Creation, to linger and meditate therein, and with minds washed clean from opinions to study it in purity and integrity. For this is that sound and language which went forth into all lands, and did not incur the confusion of Babel; this should men study to be perfect in, and becoming again as little children condescend to take the alphabet of it into their hands, and spare no pains to search and unravel the interpretation thereof.[29]

But Bacon's bookish metaphors in this passage actually serve not to unite but to separate, to distinguish Nature's pure forms of expression from man's corrupted ones. This is consistent with his belief that the prism of language has caused Nature to be seen through a glass darkly and distortedly, as in the schoolmen's failures to recognize their own word-splitting preoccupations in what they took to be God's workings in Nature. Despite his employment of literary metaphors, therefore, Bacon is anxious to keep Nature free of language. Free even of religious language—for whether his famous desire to "render unto faith the things that are faith's" is an attempt to safeguard religion from science

29. Quoted by Elizabeth Sewell in *The Orphic Voice* (New Haven, 1960), pp. 146–147.

or just the reverse is debateable, it is clear that for him the Book of Nature must be kept on a different shelf from the Book of Books. "Sacred theology," he says in *De augmentis scientiarum* (Bk. 10), "must be drawn from the word and oracles of God, not from the light of nature, or the dictates of reason." The Book of Nature, that is, must not be read symbolically, as an allegory of God, but literally, its meanings defined within their own terrestrial context.

Thus if nature is in any sense a "book" for Bacon, it is a book whose title must be reduced to lower-case letters. The next step in the devaluation of language can be found in Galileo's *Il Saggiatore*, where nature is still referred to as a book but as one whose import passeth ordinary understanding:

> Philosophy is written in that most august book, which for ever stands open before our eyes (I mean the universe) but which we cannot understand if we do not first learn to understand the language, and familiarize ourselves with the characters in which it is written. It is written in the language of mathematics, and the characters are triangles, circles, and other geometric figures, by means of which alone it is possible, humanly speaking, to understand a word of it. Without this, there can be nothing but a useless twisting and turning in a dark labyrinth.[30]

With this we move firmly into a Cartesian world of "clear and distinct ideas"—an unspeaking, and to

30. Curtius mentions this Galilean development (*European Literature and the Latin Middle Ages*, p. 324), but the quote is from Elizabeth Sewell, *The Human Metaphor* (South Bend, Ind., 1964), p. 66.

many an unspeakable, world formulated in mathematics. What is expressible in mathematics—such as Galileo's ultimates of figure, position, motion, and rest, or, more recently, molecular and atomic structures—is real, what is not is unreal or irrelevant. Thus for ordinary nonmathematical men, reality recedes, nature goes into hiding on the insides of things, and language must rest content with the leavings of science, the vain appearances. As this suggests, and as R. F. Jones has demonstrated, the rise of empiricism was not just a matter of introducing mathematics and scientific method into the history of thought; if empiricism added onto, it also subtracted from—and what it sought to subtract was language as a mode of articulating reality.[31]

Verbal skepticism, however, was by no means a seventeenth-century invention. Though there has been some dispute over Plato's true position in the *Cratylus* —Bacon for instance, as well as some modern linguists, feeling that Plato believed in a logical bond between names and their referents—he seems fairly clearly to have felt, as one would expect, that like all other sublunary things words have but a shadowy status. Thus Socrates tells the gullible Cratylus, "How real existence is to be studied or discovered is, I suspect, beyond you and me. But we may admit so much, that the knowledge of things is not to be derived from names."[32] At any rate, there is no doubt about Aris-

31. Jones, "Science and Language in England of the Mid-Seventeenth Century," (see note 1 above).
32. "Cratylus" (439), trans. Benjamin Jowett in Edith Hamilton and Huntington Cairns, eds., *Plato, the Collected Dialogues* (Princeton, 1961), p. 473. This statement by

totle's view of the matter. In his essay *On Interpretation* he declared quite matter of factly that words are conventional symbols quite distinct from the things they name. An early medieval writer like John of Salisbury could argue, in his *Metalogicon* (1159), that names were "stamped on all substances" so that there was a divinely created communion between man's mind, his world, and his language; but the fourteenth-century nominalists ran Occam's razor between words and reality, renewing the antique skepticism.[33]

Verbal skepticism in Elizabethan England, however, had little basis in classical or medieval philosophy. A more pervasive source was Puritanism, for while the Puritans did language a certain honor by regarding preaching as the high way to grace, they themselves took the low road of style. Painted eloquence was eschewed in favor of a plain delivery of the Word. This is a far cry from the preaching of Anglicans like Hooker, Andrewes, or Donne, whose variously baroque styles

---

"Socrates" has been led up to by an extended spoof of a phonomimetic origin of language in which "Socrates," blandly accepting the naive Cratylus's belief that words mirror things, persuades the skeptical Hermogenes of the "truth" of this view by means of a dazzling exhibition of inventive etymology. The dialogue, however, is long and confusing, and it is easy to see why Bacon could take Plato's ("Socrates's") fantastic etymologies straight and hence believe him to be an advocate of the logical rightness of words.

33. John of Salisbury, *Metalogicon*, trans. Daniel D. McGarry (Berkeley and Los Angeles, 1959), p. 39. See the excellent chapter on "Rhetoric, Grammar, and the Conception of Language as a Substantial Medium" by Gerald R. Bruns in his *Modern Poetry and the Idea of Language* (see note 1 above), esp. pp. 33–35.

implicitly cherished the words in which *the* Word was conveyed. As Eliot says of Lancelot Andrewes's high-pressure erudition in dealing with biblical texts: "Andrewes takes a word and derives the world from it; squeezing and squeezing the word until it yields a full juice of meaning which we should never have supposed any word to possess."[34] The Puritan verbal ideal would require words to be as self-effacing as the bread and wine at an Anglican communion, disappearing so that a luminous body of divine meaning could shine through. Thus if Bacon required a literal reading of the Book of Nature, fundamentalist Puritans demanded a literal reading of the Book of Books. The word's multiple modes of meaning, as in Dante's polysemous hierarchies, are ruthlessly leveled to a single plane of straight sense.

Puritanism and empiricism meet in a common distaste for vanities of speech. If the symbolic finery of Catholic and High Anglican language provoked the Puritans to strip words down to a core of plain sense, the pursuit of a moving and bejeweled eloquence by sixteenth-century rhetoricians drove Bacon into a temporary alliance with Aristotle:

> It seems to me that Pygmalion's frenzy is a good emblem or portraiture of this vanity [of hunting more after words than matter]: for words are but the images of matter, and except they have life of reason and invention, to fall in love with them is all one as to fall in love with a picture.[35]

34. T. S. Eliot, *Selected Essays, 1917–1932* (New York, 1932), p. 295.

35. Francis Bacon, *Of the Advancement of Learning,* Book 1, 3, in *The Advancement of Learning and New At-*

Bacon's use of "Pygmalion's frenzy" as an "emblem" typifies his linguistic dualism. At first glance it seems curious that he should prefer what he calls "poesie allusive" to his other primary modes, "poesie narrative" and "poesie representative" (in *The Advancement of Learning*, Bk. 2, 4). A reformer who wants language correlated to reality and an empiricist who puts a premium on sensory evidence might be expected to advocate realistic literature ("poesie representative") and to shy away from "allusive" allegories that do scant justice to sensible things. But in his leanings toward allegory, as with Pygmalion's frenzy, Bacon remains quite faithful both to reason and to the scientific ideal of a transparent language, insofar as allegory invites us to see through words and poems to a rational structure of meaning on the other side. The best example of this in Bacon is his *The Wisdom of the Ancients* where he

---

lantis, ed. Thomas Case (London, 1906), p. 40. It is interesting that Bacon's view of words as "images of matter" reappears in Wittgenstein's *Tractatus Logico-Philosophicus* in the argument that all discourse can be reduced to atomic propositions that are "pictures" of facts or things. The assumption that language has essentially this one photographic function is radically modified later on in Wittgenstein's *Philosophical Investigations* where he holds that language has no single essence, photographic or other, but consists of endlessly diverse "games" in which words play now one role, now another. This position is obviously more acceptable to the literary critic, who has always acknowledged the varying claims made on words by different modes of discourse, by different genres, poems, and even lines within poems. If Wittgenstein came round to saying "Don't ask for the meaning, ask for the use," literary critics have long had their own version of this: "Don't ask for the meaning, ask for the context."

patiently and ingeniously dissects thirty-one fables to extract their wisdom.

Bacon's interest in the ideas conveyed by emblem and allegory is consistent with his more general belief —shared by Plato, Aristotle, and the medieval nominalists—that words express concepts rather than objects. The ontological view of language, derived from *Genesis* and held by neoplatonists, cabbalists, the gnostic tradition, all reputable magicians, and most orthodox Elizabethans, assumed that the names of things had a divine imprimatur and that language as a whole was simply a vast collection of names, a vocabulary of the world. Throughout the seventeenth century, however, two main developments occurred. The empirical philosophers and the Royal Society in England, Descartes and the Port Royal grammarians in France, and Leibniz later on in Germany, all recognized in varying degrees, first, that words reflected not things themselves but men's concepts of things and, second, that the relation between word and concept is arbitrary. If words are indeed distinct from the things they name, then truth must be sought not in language, but, as Bacon felt, by putting Nature on the rack and extorting her secrets through experiment, observation, and a judicial weighing of the evidence.[36] His shift of emphasis from words to things is commemorated in a wondrous poem by Abraham Cowley prefacing Thomas Sprat's *History of the Royal Society* (1667), one stanza of which deserves rescuing from Oblivion's poke:

36. See Ernst Cassirer, *The Platonic Renaissance in England* (Austin, Texas, 1953), pp. 46–48, for a discussion of Bacon's experimental method as inquisitorial.

From words, which are but Pictures of the Thought,
(Though we our Thoughts from them perversely drew)
To Things, the Mind's right Object, he it brought:
Like foolish Birds to painted Grapes we flew;
He sought and gathered for our Use the true;
And when on Heaps the chosen Bunches lay,
He pressed them wisely the mechanic Way,
Till all their Juice did in one Vessel join,
Ferment into a Nourishment Divine,
    The thirsty Soul's refreshing Wine.

Hobbes too, in his radical nominalism, regarded words as merely the marks of things, no more inherently valuable or meaningful than mathematical symbols. In fact, in wisdom's employ, words have a most arithmetical look about them: "For words," he says, "are wise mens counters, they do but reckon by them." That "reckon" may seem only metaphoric until we move to the next sentence: *Subject to Names,* is whatsoever can enter into, or be considered in an account; and be added one to another to make a summe; or subtracted one from another, and leave a remainder."[37] Unlike Bacon, Hobbes realized that "True and False are attributes of Speech, not of Things," but

37. Thomas Hobbes, *Leviathan,* ed. C. B. MacPherson (Baltimore, 1968), 1:4:106. In Hobbes's discussion of words, mathematical metaphors—"cast up sums," "reckoning," "multiply," "keep account of," "summing up," and so on—are everywhere in evidence. Indeed his view of scientific method and knowledge is based on an additive notion. One first imposes names on things, then adds names together to get assertions, then adds assertions together to get syllogisms, and so on "till we come to a knowledge of all the Consequences of names appertaining to the subject in hand; and that it is, men call SCIENCE" (p. 115).

speech can lead to truth only if it jettisons everything figurative, abstract, and ambiguous and proceeds with the rigor and exactitude of mathematical calculation.

Bacon's and Hobbes's insistence on purifying language became institutionalized in the Royal Society, which had as one of its projects, soon abandoned, the reform of the English tongue. In his *History of the Royal Society* (1667), Thomas Sprat points out what can be done stylistically, in the absence of a fully reconstituted language, to minimize the corruptions of speech:

> [The members of the Society] have therefore been most rigorous in putting into execution the only Remedy that can be found for this extravagance: and that has been, a constant Resolution, to reject all the amplifications, digressions, and swellings of style: to return back to the primitive purity and shortness, when men delivered so many *things*, almost in equal number of *words*. They have exacted from all their members a close, naked, natural way of speaking; positive expressions; clearness; a native easiness; bringing all things as near the *Mathematical plainness* as they can.[38]

Sprat offers here the scientific equivalent to the Puritan advocacy of the plain style as the properly self-effacing means of delivering divine truths. Such a passion for plainness was to reach its pitch of perfection not in the Royal Society, alas, but in the Grand Academy of Lagado, in Book 3 of *Gulliver's Travels*. Content with no halfway measures in gaining direct access to reality,

38. Thomas Sprat, *History of the Royal Society* (London, 1667), p. 113.

Swift's *virtuosi* abandon words entirely in favor of the things themselves, which they haul about on their backs and, in moments of communicative zeal, fetch forth to display to one another. This, as Gulliver observes, is an altogether satisfactory practice for short conversations, but something of a bother "if a man's business be very great and of various kinds." In Lagado the mind of a genius must have beneath it the back of a giant or else go ingloriously mute.

The *reductio ad res* of Lagado reflects the seventeenth-century belief that warped notions about nature arise from men's failure to distinguish words from things. As Descartes said in his second Meditation, "Words often impede me and I am almost deceived by the terms of ordinary language." A familiar complaint among philosophers. Wittgenstein said that "philosophy is a battle against the bewitchment of our intelligence by means of language," and Bertrand Russell labeled this bewitchment "the fallacy of verbalism [which] consists in mistaking the properties of words for the properties of things."[39]

One way of circumventing this fallacy in the seventeenth century is expressed by Thomas Sprat, as quoted above: rid speech of its imperfections, reduce it to a native simplicity, shine up the lens of language to a high gloss so that one may see reality through it without distortion. But what if the ordinary languages of English, French, German, for instance were hopelessly corrupt? Two remedies presented themselves; one

39. Ludwig Wittgenstein, *Philosophical Investigations* (Oxford, 1963), p. 47e. Bertrand Russell, "Vagueness," *Australasian Journal of Psychology and Philosophy* 1 (1923): 85.

could go backward or forward. Linguistic antiquarians like Camden, Verstegan, Goropius, and Athanasius Kircher went backward, hoping in some measure to recover the lost Edenic speech at a point before corruption set in. Failure to reconstruct the *lingua humana*, however, persuaded other more inventive linguists to fashion artificial substitutes quite divorced from all past languages. What was needed, it was felt, was a universal language based on rational principles. Sprat's concern for mathematical plainness, for instance, inspired Cave Beck to propose a scientific language in which numbers would substitute for letters and syllables *(Universal Character, 1657)*. He was followed by George Dalgardo, whose *Ars Signorum* appeared in 1661, and by the most ambitious of all, John Wilkins, who in his famous *Essay towards a Real Character and Philosophical Language* (1668), essayed to classify everything in the universe and then to invent a symbol to denote its genus and species.

*

These seventeenth-century developments have a decidedly modern look. Sprat's anxieties about plainness and clarity of expression in his time are reflected today in the so-called "ordinary language philosophy," centered in Oxford and descended from the Wittgenstein of the *Philosophical Investigations*. Similarly, the attempts to fashion a universal symbolism in the seventeenth century have their twentieth-century analogues in the "formalized languages" constructed by logical positivists. Both schools proceed upon the notion that there is no underlying bond between natural language and reality. It is abundantly clear that the domain of the word has shrunk, that language no longer keeps the keys of truth. The modern Book of Nature is written, as Galileo predicted, in the cryptograms of mathematics. The most fundamental features of the modern world—the atomic structure of matter, the relativity of space-time, the wave-particle character of energy—are virtually inaccessible to words. It is beyond imagining that the Department of Agriculture would versify its manuals, as Hesiod and Vergil did to express the hard truths of farming. It is no less incredible that a particle physicist would write a paper about *leptons* or *quarks* in the kind of natural language used by Democritus. As George Steiner has said:

> One *cannot* talk of transfinite numbers except mathematically; one *should not,* suggests Wittgenstein, talk of ethics or aesthetics within the presently available categories of discourse. And it is, I think, exceedingly difficult to speak meaningfully of a Jackson Pollock painting or a composition by Stockhausen. The circle has narrowed tremendously, for was there anything under heaven, be it science, metaphysics, art, or music, of which a Shakespeare, a Donne, and a Milton could not speak naturally, to which their words did not have natural access?[40]

Shakespeare wrote at a time when for most people the bond between words and the world was still intact, when language was in the natural grain of experienced life. Yet we have only to glance from Sir Thomas Elyot to Sir Francis Bacon to sense the beginnings of verbal recession, to see the large process of linguistic dissolu-

40. George Steiner, *Language and Silence* (New York, 1967), pp. 24–25.

tion writ small. The turbulence of such a time is registered in Shakespeare's *Henriad*, phrased not in the discursive characters of linguistic philosophy but in the enduring accents of dramatic art. What Shakespeare says about language is less our concern than what Shakespeare's interest in language says about Shakespearean drama. If his art is in some degree about words, if the descent of royalty reflects also a fall of speech, the art itself will have the last word, the fall of his own speech the final hearing.

Index

Abstractions: and metaphor, 49n

Agrippa, Cornelius: and poetic lies, 67, 201n

Allen, D. C., 189n

Aristotle: and literary form, 105; and verbal skepticism, 211–212

Ascham, Roger: and verbal incarnation, 198

Augustine, Saint, 187, 194; and classical sign theory, 205

Bacon, Francis, 16, 25, 27n; and idols, 31; *Advancement of Learning*, 193; and Book of Nature, 208–210, 212n, 213–214, 219

Barber, C. L., 2n, 95n, 100n; and Falstaff, 102n

Barfield, Owen, 192n

Beck, Cave: and verbal reform, 218

Bible: and verbal influence, 199–200

Blake, William: and visual-verbal expression, 107n

Blanpied, John W., 3n

Boehme, Jacob: and original language, 186–187

Book of Nature, 20, 26; and language, 205–210, 219

Bromley, John C., 2n

Brooks, Cleanth, 72

Brown, Norman O., 187n

Bruns, Gerald L.: and Elizabethan language, 184n, 211n

Budge, Sir E. A. Wallis: and word myths, 185n

Burckhardt, Sigurd, 3n, 4; and Prince John, 36n; and royal succession, 67n; and Falstaff's "death," 71–72, 135; and Agincourt, 154n

Burke, Kenneth: and literary form, 111n

Cain, H. Edward, 112n

Camden, William, 189n, 218

Campbell, Lily B., 1

Cardan, Jerome, 201n

Cassirer, Ernst, 8, 18, 25n, 190n, 191, 214n

Castiglione, Baldesar, 197

Chomsky, Noam: and innate speech, 186n

Cicero, 195

Coleridge, Samuel Taylor: and imagination, 15n; and audience expectation, 117

Colish, Marcia: and Augustine, 194
Cornelius, Paul, 189n
Cowley, Abraham: and Bacon, 214–215
Crane, Milton, 101n
Cruttwell, Pattrick, 19
Curtius, Ernst Robert, 199n; and Book of Nature *topos*, 205–206, 209n

Dalgardo, George: and verbal reform, 218
Daniel, Samuel, 190n; "Musophilus," 197
Dante, Alighieri: and language, 65n
Dean, Leonard, 3, 4n
Decorum: and Falstaff, 100–102
Dee, Dr. John, 201n
Democritus: and speech, 206, 219
Descartes, René: and Book of Nature, 209, 217
Deus ex machina: and linearity, 110
Diamond, A. S., 190n

Eiron: and Hal, 120
Eliot, T. S., 212n
Elliott, Robert C., 202n
Ellis-Fermor, Una: and *Henry V*, 139
Elyot, Sir Thomas, 219
Empson, William: and double plots, 54n

Famous Victories of Henry the Fifth, 73, 118

Finnegans Wake: and circular form, 108
Frazer, Sir James G., 191n
Frye, Northrop, 79n

Galen: and speech, 206
Galileo: and Book of Nature, 209–210, 219
Goddard, Harold: and *Henry V*, 145n
Goropius Becanus, Joannes, 188, 190n, 218
Gosson, Stephen: and poetic lies, 67

Harvey, Gabriel: and language, 200–201
Haydn, Hiram, 81n
Heilman, Robert B., 72
Herder, J. G. von: and origin of language, 185n
Herodotus: and origin of speech, 187n
Hobbes, Thomas, 25; and origin of language, 185; and nominalism, 215–216
Holinshed, Raphael: and Gaultree Forest, 36
Holophrase: and early speech, 192n, 204–205
Humphrey, A. R.: and Epilogue to 2 *Henry IV*, 31n
Hunter, G. K.: and *Henry IV*, 119–120
Hunter, William B., 81n

Interior dramatist: and Hal, 116ff.

Index

James, Henry: and visual-verbal expression, 107n
Jenkins, Harold, 112–114
Jesperson, Otto, 190n, 192n
John of Salisbury: and language, 211
Johnson, Samuel, 112
Jones, Richard Foster: and Elizabethan language, 184n, 188, 190n, 210
Julius Caesar, 206–207
Jung, Carl, 191n

Kahler, Erich, 191n
Keller, Helen, 191
Kernan, Alvin B., 1, 4; and *Henry V*, 140, 173n
Kinnell, Galway, 207
Kircher, Athanasius, 188, 218
Knights, L. C.: and *Henry V*, 142n
Knoepflmacher, U. C., 81n
Krieger, Murray: and formal unity, 146–147
Kris, Ernst, 44, 100n

La Guardia, Eric, 3, 13n; and Falstaff, 42n; and *Henry V*, 179n
Langer, Suzanne, 190n, 191
Language: and land, 33; as collective lie, 49; and entropy, 65–67; and *Henry V*, 164–169; and Elizabethan England, 183–220; and religious faith, 198–200; and Elizabethan satire, 200–201; and word

magic, 201–203; and Puritanism, 211ff.
Lévy-Bruhl, Lucien, 191n
Lie: and poetry, 67, 201n; and 1 *Henry IV*, 69ff.; at Shrewsbury, 88–89; and Falstaff, 89ff.; and ending of 1 *Henry IV*, 115–116
Linearity: and literary form, 105–110; and *Henry IV*, 111–133
Lingua Adamica, 186, 189
Lingua humana, 186
Love's Labour's Lost, 42; and word games, 44; and Pistol, 98

Mahood, Molly: and Elizabethan language, 184n
Malinowski, Bronislaw, 191n
Manheim, Michael, 2n
Mask: and Falstaff, 103–104; and Hal, 104
Meiosis: and Hal, 52
Merleau-Ponty, Maurice: and innate speech, 186n
Metadrama: in *The Henriad*, 5–9
Metaphor: and artistic projection, 5; and *Richard II*, 12–13, 17ff.; and the linguistic system, 14ff.; and verbal error, 15–16; and Falstaff, 45–46; and abstractions, 49n; and kingship, 50ff.; and the lie, 50, 53; and double plots, 54ff.; and theater in *Henry V*, 135–136

Index

Mimesis: and *1 Henry IV,* 73ff.

Mitchell, Charles: and *Henry V,* 152n

More, Sir Thomas: and disorder, 38–39

Müller, Max, 192n

Names: and kingship, 5–6; and identity in *Richard II,* 17–18; and Hotspur, 57; and titles of honor, 89ff.; and things, 201–202

Nashe, Thomas: and Elizabethan language, 200–201

Nicholson, Marjorie, 206n

"Ode on a Grecian Urn," 106n

Olivier, Laurence: and *Henry V,* 142n

Ong, Walter: and rhetoric, 171n; and Elizabethan language, 184n, 192n

Order: and Falstaff, 40; political and dramatic, 122ff.; and *Henry V,* 134–155

Ornstein, Robert, 2n

Palmer, John, 2n, 152n

Paracelsus: and names, 201–202, 206n

Peacham, Henry, 200

Pei, Mario, 202n

Picard, Max: and original language, 188

Pierce, Robert B., 2n

Plato: and the *Cratylus,* 210–211

Prior, Moody E., 2n; and *Henry V,* 141–142, 145n

Puritanism: and language, 211ff.; and empiricism, 212–213

Puttenham, George, 15

Reese, M. M., 2n

Rhetoric: in *Henry V,* 171–173, 179–180

Ribner, Irving, 2n

Richmond, H. M., 2n

Righter, Anne: and Pistol, 98n

Romeo and Juliet: and verbal skepticism, 30

Rossi, Paolo, 31n

Rossiter, A. P., 2n

Royal Society, 25; and language, 216

Russell, Bertrand, 217

Sapir-Whorf hypothesis, 26–27

Scaliger, Joseph Justus, 197

Sewell, Arthur, 85n

Sewell, Elizabeth, 208n, 209n

Shaaber, M. A., 112, 119–120

Shakespearean Metadrama, 42n

Sidney, Sir Philip, 197

Spitzer, Leo, 206n

Sprat, Thomas: and Royal Society, 214; and verbal reform, 216–218

Index

Steiner, George, 219

Stevens, Wallace, 207

Stewart, J. I. M., 44, 100n

Stribrny, Z., 2n

Style: and Hal, 83–85, 100–101

Succession: and kingship, 63–64; and verbal creativity, 64–67

Sussmilch, Johann P.: and origin of speech, 185n

Swadesh, Morris, 190n

Swift, Jonathan: and Houyhnhnms, 27–28; and verbal skepticism, 216–217

Symbolism: and *The Henriad*, 3–5

Synechdoche: and *Henry V*, 136–137

Tempest, The: and presentational time, 109–110; and Caliban, 200

Theater: and *Henry V*, 174–178

Tillyard, E. M. W., 1, 19

Time: and *Richard II*, 10–11; and Falstaff, 41

Toliver, Harold E., 3

Traversi, Derek, 2

Troilus and Cressida, 21

Tudor Homilies, 20

Twelfth Night: and verbal skepticism, 30

Unity: and dramatic form, 146ff.

Upton, John, 112

Verstegan, Richard, 189n, 218

Visual Design: and aesthetic statement, 105–110

Vivas, Eliseo, 8

Walter, J. H., 135

Webbe, William, 195n

Webber, Joan, 3, 101n; and King Harry, 153n; and *Henry V*, 173n

Wheelwright, Philip, 20n

Whorf, Benjamin, 26–27

Wilkins, John: and linguistic reform, 218

Williams, Philip, 100n

Wilson, J. Dover, 1, 81n

Wilson, Richard A., 190n

Wilson, Thomas: and rhetoric, 196–197, 200

Winny, J., 2n

Winters, Yvor: and imitative form, 147

Wittgenstein, Ludwig: and Bacon, 213n; 217–218

Words: and meanings, 22–23, 26–27

Yeh, Max: and origin of speech, 187n

Young, David: and 2 *Henry IV*, 135n